THE BIG LITTLE BOOK OF tarot

THE BIG LITTLE BOOK OF tarot

The only book you'll ever need

RACHEL POLLACK

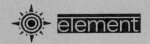

Element
An Imprint of HarperCollins*Publishers*
77–85 Fulham Palace Road,
Hammersmith,
London W6 8JB

The website address is: www.thorsonselement.com

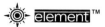

and *Element* are trademarks of
HarperCollins*Publishers* Limited

Previously published as
Complete Illustrated Guide to Tarot by Element Books
This edition published by Element 2004

10 9 8 7 6 5 4 3 2 1

A catalogue record for this book is
available from the British Library

ISBN 0 00 716679 6

Printed and bound by Imago

NOTE FROM THE PUBLISHER
Any information given in this book is not intended to be taken
as a replacement for medical advice. Any person with a
condition requiring medical attention should consult a qualified
practitioner or therapist.

contents

what is tarot?

The 78 cards of the Tarot have lived many lives in the 600 years that we have known them — a card game played by the Italian nobility, works of fine art, allegories of moral teachings and philosophy, inspiration for novels and films, coded systems for magic and esoteric wisdom, gateways for meditation, and much more. Most of all, however, we know the Tarot for its use in divination. Divination is the quest for supernatural knowledge of the past, present, and future. Many methods of divination have been utilized by different cultures throughout the centuries, and cartomancy, or the use of cards for fortune-telling, dates back many centuries. It was in the late 18th century, however, that the use of Tarot cards for divination became widespread. We now use Tarot readings in an attempt to understand ourselves better and maybe even discover the future.

The practice of divination of one kind or another ranks among humanity's oldest and most honored of activities. Virtually every culture has developed some method of using symbolic systems to help them discover secrets beyond ordinary sources of information. People have studied the patterns and cries of birds, or cut the birds open to study their entrails. The Ancient Chinese heated iron rods and set them against the shells of dead tortoises to see what images appeared when the shells cracked. European women turn over teacups to discover what pictures of the future are revealed in the tea leaves clinging to their porcelain.

divination

1

In our modern world, we have tended to denigrate divination as irrational, and so push it to the margins of society. We think of Tarot readers as women in flashy clothes who will tell your fortune in a storefront. Other societies, however, have placed divination at the core of their cultural and religious activities. In Ancient Greece, people traveled great distances to consult the oracle at Delphi, a place the Greeks called "the navel of the world." Stephen Karcher, the translator of the *I Ching*, the Chinese *"Book of Changes,"* has written that the *I Ching* formed the very center of spirituality in China. In many parts of Africa, the divination system that is known as Ifa remains the primary way in which the Orishas, or gods, reveal their divine presence in everyday human life.

A carved bowl used by the people of Africa as part of their divination rituals.

"Divination" derives from the Latin word *divinatio,* to divine. Whatever the method, when we do a divination we seek to understand, in some small way, the spiritual patterns that underlie our lives. Divination systems, especially the more elaborate ones, almost always reflect a religious or philosophical system. We may read the Tarot as a party game, but the game works because the symbols on the Tarot cards describe the deeper truths that give meaning to our lives.

And it works because the Tarot consists of pictures rather than words. While it is true that people have written hundreds of books about the Tarot, and that most people who want to use the cards in a reading look up their meanings in a book such as this one, the Tarot remains first and foremost pictures – mysterious, evocative, suggestive of whole worlds of meaning.

The *I Ching* has revealed the flow of events and individual lives for thousands of years.

People have always expressed the greatest truths in pictures. European art begins some 30,000 years ago, with the powerful cave paintings of bulls and other animals that have been discovered in France and Spain.

The Chinese looked deeply into the spiritual meanings of divination.

No one knows the exact purpose of these oldest works of art. Theories regarding their meaning usually assume some kind of magic, or initiation ceremonies. Considering how widespread divination is, perhaps the cave painters were establishing a system of images for "readings."

A European System

If most cultures create some system of divination, and all these systems express spiritual ideas, they nevertheless differ from one to another. These differences derive from the different cultures that developed them. The *I Ching* "hexagrams" carry the special qualities and beliefs of

China, while the "praise-poems" of Ifa reveal the unique African way of looking at the world.

The Tarot is the most European of all divination systems. Its scenes include popes and jugglers, hermits and fools, along with kings and queens and their attendant knights and pages. Some scenes come from religion, such as the Last Judgment, with the angel Gabriel blowing his horn for the dead to rise from their graves. The Devil himself makes an appearance, as does the cherubic figure of Cupid, about to shoot an arrow into an unsuspecting young man.

Ancient European cave paintings may have developed a language of images.

Other cards portray allegorical scenes once very well known to the educated European people but now more obscure and therefore mysterious. Even the card of Death, so popular in movies about Tarot readings, once taught an allegorical lesson. It showed Death as a skeleton harvesting the heads of kings as well as peasants, and so reminding us that whatever our position in life we all must die.

Death shows no mercy to either prince or pauper.

Over time, many of these allegorical scenes became less commonplace and more dominant. Esoteric ideas became more dominant. The cards have taken on the meaning of a story, that of the soul's journey, from birth through the various trials and challenges of life, and finally to death and perhaps resurrection. Interwoven with this story we can find threads of initiation and mystic enlightenment.

The traditional Tarot deck consists of 78 cards, divided into two parts, the trump cards and the suits, otherwise known as the Major Arcana (or Greater Arcana) and the Minor Arcana (or Lesser Arcana). Arcana is a Latin word meaning "secrets." The Major Arcana, or trumps, are the cards unique to the Tarot deck, with their allegorical pictures and their titles such as "the Magician" or "The Hanged Man" or "The Devil."

the tarot's structure

2

The word "trump" derives from the Italian word *trionf* or "triumph," for in the game of Tarot these cards will capture, or triumph over, the ordinary cards of the four suits.

Twenty-two in number (0 plus 1 to 21), these are the cards that have provoked so many theories and speculations throughout the years. Where the Renaissance Tarot decks showed dramatic or elegant figures, many of the more modern ones stress both extremely stylized images and very specific symbolism.

Despite the great variety of images, the titles and basic illustrations of the Major Arcana have remained remarkably consistent through the centuries. There is actually a classic, or standard, set of Major Arcana images, a French deck known as the Tarot de Marseilles, whose designs we can trace back to the 16th century. The later occult decks have almost all based their pictures and symbolic ideas on this famous deck. The modern occult tradition began in France and it was natural for the French interpreters to use the deck they thought of as "original." And yet, the Tarot de Marseilles actually appears very different from the oldest decks we know, which date from Italy in the mid-15th century. We can look at the Sun card for an example. We can find a great deal of symbolic meaning in the Marseilles

The contemporary Elemental Tarot evokes the quality of Wind through stylized images and symbols.

This "wild" joker from conventional playing cards hints at the same freedom symbolized in the much older Fool of the Tarot.

image of two children holding hands in a garden. But when we look at the oldest Tarot deck known, the so-called "Visconti-Sforza" *(see opposite),* which dates from c. 1475, we find a very different picture on the card – a winged child, or cherub, flying with a glowing head held aloft.

The Major Arcana cards have received the most attention primarily because of their clearly allegorical pictures. Until very recently, most interpretative books on the Tarot have given much less notice to the actual bulk of the deck – the 56 cards of the Minor Arcana (their very name demonstrates their low regard). These are the cards of the four suits, very similar to the playing cards that most of us have known since our childhood. Indeed, in Spain and some other countries ordinary playing cards have the same suit emblems as the Tarot deck – Wands (or Staves), Cups, Swords, and Coins (or Disks). In Anglo-Saxon countries (and many other countries besides), Wands have become Clubs, Cups Hearts, Swords Spades, and Coins Diamonds.

Each suit consists of almost the same cards as its equivalent in bridge or poker decks: Ace through ten plus a group of court cards. Where regular playing cards have three of these court figure cards – Jack, Queen, and King – the Tarot deck has four – Page (the Jack), Knight, Queen, and King.

Right
These two ways of showing the power of the sun both feature children.

Some people believe that just as the trump cards may have begun as allegorical lessons, so the four suit emblems may signify the four main social classes in medieval Europe. The

Staves represent the peasants who work in the fields and forests. The Cups belong to the priesthood, who use chalices in the mass. Swords clearly represent the nobility, while Coins just as obviously signify the merchants (one problem with this is the presence of ruling court cards in each suit).

For a long time students of Tarot believed that modern playing cards derived from the Tarot deck. The Knights dropped out and the trumps disappeared except for the Fool, which became the modern Joker, and behold, ordinary playing cards emerged, still carrying within them their secret origin. Historical research, however, does suggest that both decks, regular cards and the Tarot, originated at about the same time and evolved alongside each other.

The Joker in a pack of regular playing cards apparently does not descend directly from the Tarot Fool. Instead, some members of a New York gentlemen's poker club invented the card in the 19th century to make the game more exciting. And yet, this story demonstrates the power of allegorical symbols. The card image they chose, that of a court jester, does not exactly match the classic Tarot Fool, usually shown as a wanderer or a tramp or a beautiful boy. The term Fool, however, was often used for jesters (as, for example, in the character that appears in William Shakespeare's play *King Lear)* and "wise fools" often acted like human wild cards in such settings as medieval carnivals, where the celebrants crowned a King of Fools to rule over their revelry and recklessness.

The trumps receive so much attention because of their mystery. Conversely, the suit cards have been ignored because of their plainness. Until the 20th century (and in many modern decks as well) virtually all Tarots showed only schematic designs for the so-called "pip" cards, the Ace to Ten in each suit. For example, the Four of Swords would show four swords in an elaborate or geometric pattern, the Eight of Cups eight cups arranged on the card, and so on.

the opening of the minor arcana

The designs tended to be more elaborate than those on playing cards, but without any suggestion of symbolism. The cards did not invite much esoteric interpretation, and to use them for divination required a reader to memorize a set of simple formulas.

All this changed in the 20th century. The Hermetic Order of the Golden Dawn *(see pages 63–71)* opened the way with slightly more elaborate designs and extra titles for the pip cards, such as "Lord of Material Gain." Two of its members, however, took the pip cards much further. In 1909 the Rider company of England published a Tarot deck that was designed by Arthur Edward Waite and painted by Pamela Colman Smith. Waite gave most of his attention to certain changes in the Major Arcana. In the long run, however, the Rider Pack's greatest significance lay in Pamela Colman Smith's revolutionary Minor Arcana. For the first time an actual scene appeared on every card.

In his book on the Tarot deck, Waite used traditional divinatory formulas for the pip cards. For example, for the Six of Swords

Above
The Golden Dawn Six of Swords opens the way to symbolic interpretation.

Left
Any symbolism in this Marseilles pip card is very subtle and elusive.

card he gave the following meanings "Journey by water, route, way, envoy, commissionary, expedient." As time went on and the Rider Pack became the bestselling Tarot of all time, many readers began to look more deeply into the Minor pictures. That Six of Swords may suggest a journey of dead souls across the River Styx in Greek mythology, or a family carrying secrets and burdens through the generations, or simply a quiet passage to a new life. By including scenes on every card the Rider Pack opened the Minor Arcana to more complex interpretations. As a result, a large number of contemporary decks base their Minor Arcana on Pamela Smith's original drawings.

Universal Waite Six of Swords card takes us into a dream-like story.

The pip cards may invite more interpretation than in earlier times, but the court cards remain something of a problem. Many Tarot readers, and not only beginners, find the court cards the most difficult to interpret. Do they represent people in the person's life? Or the person? Do they signify special qualities, or just physical appearance? One reason for this difficulty is the court cards' static quality. How much can we say, really, about kings and queens sitting on their thrones, or knights charging on their horses? Traditionally they do indeed represent actual people, but we still need the other cards in the reading to indicate to us what exactly those people are doing.

In order to liven up these cards and give them more meaning, modern decks have varied their pictures and even their names. The Golden Dawn changed the titles to King,

Queen, Prince, and Princess, with the romantic suggestion that the King comes in to woo the Queen and together they create the Prince and Princess. The esoteric order of the Golden Dawn also dramatized the pictures to increase their symbolic values. The Queen of Swords, for example, shows a woman holding a severed head, like the Old Testament heroine Judith, who took the head of Israel's enemy.

Some decks, such as the Voyager Tarot, have changed the court cards to depict stages in a person's life. The Voyager shows us Sage, Woman, Man, and Child. Notice that in this deck, as in the Golden Dawn system, male and female are balanced, unlike the traditional Page, Knight, Queen, and King. A few decks have taken an even more radical approach and done away with the idea of court cards altogether. Shining Woman Tarot replaces the characters with Place, Knower, Gift, and Speaker – cards that depict a spiritual progress through life.

Other decks have turned to mythology for the court cards. The Mythological Tarot uses characters from Ancient Greece to fill the traditional roles. The Haindl Tarot translates the idea of "court" from a royal domain to the courtyard of a family, with Mother, Father, Daughter, and Son. The pictures, however, show gods and goddesses from different cultures for each suit in an attempt to represent the world through four sacred traditions. Similarly, the Daughters of the Moon deck uses the court cards to portray a gallery of goddesses.

QUEEN OF SWORDS

This Golden Dawn card startles us with its apparent violence. It may represent the idea of conquering the ego.

The contemporary Tarot has evolved into a tradition that allows for many variations. The esoteric Tarot remains alive and stronger than ever, with decks that come heavily laden with symbolism. Where previous occult decks attempted to conceal their meanings ("occult" means "hidden") more recent esoteric decks often mark each card with a dizzying array of symbols, from alchemy to Hebrew letters to astrology to the *I Ching*. The Italian artist Giorgio Tavaglione attempted to synthesize a range of teachings in his lavishly painted Stairs of Gold Tarot. While the occult tradition flourishes, the Tarot has opened new territory. Some decks are primarily works of art, such as the Salvador Dali Tarot, with collages that borrow from the history of Western art.

the modern tarot

4

One of the most unusual of the Tarot "decks" is the magnificent sculpture garden of Niki de St. Phalle, whose brightly colored statues, covered in ceramics or mirrors, reach high above the trees in their Southern Tuscany setting.

Other Tarot decks have sought to adapt the European background to varied cultures.

In one of the earliest of such works, the Native American Tarot, the cards vividly illustrate the mythology and social structure of Native North American peoples. Another deck from the 1970s, the Xultun Maya Tarot, portrayed its figures in the style of pre-Columbian art. Since then, the Tarot world has seen Japanese and Chinese Tarots, a Tarot based on a medieval Finnish epic, Viking Tarots, Gipsy and Russian Tarots, and so on.

The dazzling Stairs of Gold Tarot by Italian artist Giorgio Tavaglione.

Some of these decks seek primarily to illustrate the cultural history or legends of a particular people. Others wish to use the Tarot to bring to life a spiritual teaching, in the way that the traditional Tarot deck gives life to the Western Hermetic system of developing the self. For instance, the Tarot of the Orishas allows the gods and goddesses of West African religion to emerge in lush paintings. The directions for using this deck not only give the meanings of the cards, they also instruct the reader in the African belief system and some of its ritual practices. With the stimulation of the pictures a reader can learn to invoke the Orishas in her or his life.

The popularity of Tarot has led to the creation of decks that illustrate other divinatory systems. Both the *I Ching* and the Scandinavian Runes have their own sets of images, and yet both have seen various card decks that transform them into Tarotlike pictures. For example, the Rune Beorc is both the letter B and the symbol of a birch tree. The actual Rune consists just of the letter, traditionally inscribed on a small stone or piece of wood. A card of Beorc shows the letter but also a painting of the tree in a setting that successfully evokes its symbolic meaning.

A further development involves Tarot and women. In the history of Tarot, readers have been primarily female, partly because the practice of Tarot reading calls for the very qualities we think of as particularly feminine – intuition, psychic awareness, sensitivity and empathy. This tradition, and the Tarot's place outside the rationalist mainstream of Western culture, has made the cards very attractive to feminists who want to express the power of women's spirituality. In the early and mid-1980s several decks appeared designed by and for women.

A number of these decks were round rather than rectangular, suggesting both the female form and the image of the full Moon, whose worship many women had revived as an essential part of the Wiccan, or Witchcraft, religion. The women's Tarot decks also tended to feature goddesses and female-centered spirituality, their attachment to nature, women's relationships, including sexual as well as communal relationships, and representation of all ages, races, and body types. One of the first of these decks, the Motherpeace Tarot of Karen Vogel and Vicki Noble, has become one of the most popular decks of modern times.

In the last few decades, Tarot has emerged more and more as an art form expressing many qualities and ideas. Where once Tarot designers sought to reveal the One True Tarot, now creators of new Tarot decks often will do a group of decks, the way a painter will do many paintings or different series of works. Italian artist Elisabetta Cassari has done decks with settings ranging from the Middle Ages to outer space. Artist and art historian Brian Williams has created a number of decks that show Tarot's versatility. While the design of Williams' Renaissance Tarot draws on Classical mythology and art, his Pomo Tarot ("Pomo" is short for "postmodern") satirizes popular culture, with suits named Guns, Bottles, Money, and televisions. Most of the pictures are actually cartoon parodies of famous paintings.

Left
The Ukiyoë Tarot is based on the "floating world" of the 18th-century Japanese Ukiyoë painting style.

Below left
The Idiot from the Pomo Tarot combines a sleazy modern singer with the classic imagery for the Fool.

Below
The Motherpeace Tarot High Priestess portrays the earth-based power of women's spirituality.

High Priestess

origins and history

The legends of the origins of Tarot are many, wonderful, and diverse. Ancient Egypt, long regarded as a source of the mysterious and magical, with its secret chamber of initiations deep in a pyramid. Atlantis, where master magicians seek to preserve their wisdom before the continent sinks beneath the waves of destruction, forever lost to humankind. Wise women healers, who know they must conceal their thousand-year-old teachings from the fires of the Inquisition. Mystical rabbis, deep in ecstatic trance visions of the Tree of Life. Romany Gypsy masters of fortune telling. Moroccan mages and the Holy Grail. All these legends and more have been described as the true origin of the Tarot. And yet, on the other side, we find those individuals who insist that the Tarot is "nothing but a game," a simple pastime invented for nothing more serious than the courtly amusement of noble European ladies and gentlemen. Just where does the mysterious Tarot originate from? And how did it gain its miraculous reputation?

The occult tradition in Tarot dates back only 200 years. In that short time a remarkable number of legends have grown up around the cards. Partly this stems from the fact that nobody really knows their precise origin other than their appearance as a card game. Partly it comes from the excitement of using our imagination to create a wondrous story. And partly it derives from a need to justify the claim that the cards contain the secrets of existence, not to mention the power to reveal the future.

the legends of ancient egypt

Obviously, the emotional logic seems to run, something so filled with wisdom and power cannot have begun its life just a few hundred years ago as a game. It has become part of the very tradition of Tarot to give it wondrous and mysterious origins.

Many people believe that the Tarot originated in Ancient Egypt. The first Tarot occultists made this claim and the idea took hold. Egypt has always held a special place in the Western imagination. The two main sources of European culture, the Ancient Greeks and the Hebrews, both looked on Egypt as a place of great knowledge, mystery, and magic. Additionally, the Hebrews saw Egypt as a place of oppression. As a very old culture, Egypt appeared to be filled with ancient secrets and power. Before the discovery of the Rosetta Stone in the early 19th century, which allowed scholars to decipher the hieroglyphs, that colorful form of picture writing seemed to embody such power. And since the Tarot also worked in pictures, it was only natural to assume some connection between the two.

Two main legends connect the Tarot to Egypt. Both are entirely fictional. The first comes from the earliest known Tarot occultist, Antoine Court de Gébelin. He described the cards as a Book of All Knowledge created by Ancient Egyptian magicians to teach their disciples secretly without any danger of ordinary people discovering what they were doing.

The second legend describes a series of images used to initiate disciples into a direct knowledge of the gods. Remember that the Major Arcana contains 22 cards. Supposedly a temple in Egypt held a secret chamber with two lines of 11 lifesized pictures each. The disciple, suitably prepared through training, meditation, and fasting, enters the chamber. As he passes the double sets of pictures, they will impress themselves directly on his imagination. By the time he reaches the end, he will find himself transformed.

The problem with both these stories is that no evidence for them exists. Antoine Court de Gébelin

Below
The Death card from the Kashmir Tarot deck shows a journey similar to Ra's nightly voyage through darkness.

developed the idea of a secret Egyptian Book of All Knowledge after pondering a deck of Tarot playing cards shown him by a friend.

The secret temple comes from the work of a 19th-century French occultist named Paul Christian who developed a complex fiction and claimed it to be a direct translation from a 4th-century writer named Iamblichus. Supposedly quoting Iamblichus, Christian tells how the initiate climbed down a ladder with 78 rungs to enter the hall of the 22 pictures, each of which revealed truths of the divine, the intellectual, and the physical worlds.

Just as the Major Arcana contains 22 cards, so the Tarot as a whole contains 78. In a master stroke, however, Christian never mentions the Tarot in his "translation" from Iamblichus. Thus the reader who knows something of the Tarot and its occult history will read Iamblichus's supposed 4th-century text and say "Wait a moment. 78 rungs, 22 pictures – That's the Tarot!" and assume that he or she has made the essential connection and "discovered" the Tarot's Egyptian origin.

Paul Christian's fiction has become ingrained in the legend of Tarot's origins. Some contemporary books will still cite this secret temple, and Iamblichus's description of it as if they existed in the real world of history and archeology. Others, who know that Christian made it up, will still describe it as a powerful myth with a kind of truth of its own. A few people have even attempted to "re-create" the temple, using lifesized paintings of Egyptian-style Tarot cards on either side of a long narrow hall.

Because the myth of the Tarot's Egyptian origin has proven so enduring, many Tarot creators have designed Egyptian-style card decks. Some of these decks go back all the way to the 18th and 19th centuries. A few modern decks incorporate more accurate images from Egyptian mythology.

Far left
The Devil card from the Tarot of Transition depicts a monster who devours souls unworthy of the afterlife.

Left
The Emperor card from the Papus Tarot gives an Art Deco style to the Egyptian God Horus.

GYPSIES AND OTHERS

The idea that the Tarot comes from the Romany, popularly called Gypsies, derives partly from the Egyptian origin story. The word "Gypsy" comes from "Egyptian" and the idea that this much-persecuted group of people originated in Egypt.

The fact is, however, that both historical information and the Romany's own myths of their people describe them as originally from India. In their long migration, they did indeed pass through North Africa, but they did not come from there.

The Romany people included Tarot in their own system of fortune telling, from popular demand.

Many people have pointed to the fact that the Romany use Tarot cards for divination. As mentioned before, the very image of a Tarot reader is that of a "Gypsy fortune-teller" with her scarf and coins. According to scholars Ronald Decker, Thierry DePaulis, and Michael Dummett, in their history *A Wicked Pack of Cards: The Origins of the Occult Tarot*, the Romany did not actually start using Tarot cards until quite late, when they discovered that customers expected this of them!

Just as the myth of Ancient Egyptian origins has led to the design of Egyptian-style Tarots, so Romany legends have produced various "Tarot of the Gypsies." Once again, the earliest of these decks tended just to claim Gypsy connections without any real attempt to understand or depict images of the Romany culture. By contrast, at least a few modern decks use genuine Romany images.

The Knight of Wands card from the Romany-inspired Zigeuner Tarot.

The Egyptian origin story still holds an important place in Tarot mythology. There are, however, many other stories. One recent theory compares the Major Arcana to precise phases of the Moon studied thousands of years ago by Chaldean astrologers. And feminists involved in Wicca, have described the cards as remnants of coded wisdom from a woman-centered age of peace, harmony, and knowledge. As patriarchal invaders began to overrun this ancient world, the Wise Women knew they could not preserve their schools, libraries, and other centers of traditional learning. They knew as well that the conquerors would deliberately destroy any open attempts to safeguard their wisdom. They decided to keep their knowledge intact but disguised, preserved in a manner both secret and at the same time accessible to those who could recognize it. And so they invented the Tarot, a simple game to the ignorant, but a revelation of truth to those few who could understand it.

Now, this is the same idea as Antoine Court de Gébelin's intuition that the Egyptian masters preserved their ancient wisdom as a card game. This more recent idea substitutes matriarchal priestesses for male magicians.

Hecate, the ancient goddess of the witches. The knowledge and beliefs of pagan wise women may have influenced the Tarot.

Quite a few of the Tarot origin stories follow this pattern. Some people have claimed that the Tarot comes all the way from Atlantis. As the continent began to show signs of destruction, the councils of the wise knew they could not preserve their vast wisdom in its full form. They condensed this magic and truth down to an essential set of 22 pictures. Not just the individual images but the very number and structure would reveal the hidden laws of creation. Unrecognized, the pictures would pass for a simple game. The very ability to play and gamble with them would help ensure their survival, for people will always want games. For the wise, however, the pictures, with all their precise symbolism, would once more open up to reveal the treasures of Atlantis.

Tantra and the Tarot

The feminist researcher and writer Barbara Walker in her book *The Secrets of the Tarot* developed the idea that the Major Arcana with its Fool cards (zero) plus 1–21 originally derived from an ancient form of goddess worship in India, known as Tantra. The 21 numbered trumps, she says, represent the "Taras," or aspects of the Mother Goddess. This name Tara, Walker speculates, may have given the Tarot its name.

The Hindu Mother Goddess Tara has 21 aspects. Like the 21 numbered trumps in the Tarot, the Taras express practices leading to spiritual enlightenment.

Some people may think that Walker is cheating a little by separating the Fool from the other trumps to produce 21. In fact, many interpreters of Tarot, whatever their belief about its origin, have seen the Fool as separate, a symbol of the person who must encounter all the experiences shown on the other cards. Quite a few works on the Tarot have described the cards (or at least the cards that appear in the Major Arcana) as

MOROCCAN MAGES AND THE HOLY GRAIL

There is a legend of a meeting of mages in the Moroccan city of Fez in the year 1200. As the world moved to the modern age, the wise men knew that their ancient teachings would not survive. Their knowledge would become repressed, then lost in the world's many languages and cultures. Each group or school might gain a portion of the truth, but lacking the entire system of knowledge they would distort what they knew rather than preserve it. The magicians created the Tarot, a series of wordless pictures, to transcend language and individual cultures (although the images reflect European social structure). Once again, its popularity as a game would preserve it for those few who could recognize its true nature. In the late 1950s, Roland Berrill, the founder of Mensa, an organization for people with high I.Q.s, commissioned a British artist named Michael Hobdell to create the "Royal Fez Moroccan Tarot." Though they attempt to capture a Moroccan sense of design (especially in the clothes), the pictures descend directly from Smith and Waite's Rider Pack.

One further myth deserves special mention, if only because it is virtually the only one to focus more on the Minor Arcana than the Major. In the Middle Ages a cycle of stories developed around the Holy Grail, the cup used by Jesus Christ to celebrate communion at the Last Supper. St. Joseph of Arimathea used this cup to collect Christ's blood after a Roman soldier wounded him on the cross. Joseph

The Moroccan Tarot adapts the Rider Pack scenes with clothing and a background evocative of medieval Fez.

then took the chalice and the soldier's spear to England. These two objects, the cup and the spear, form the emblems for the suits of Cups and Wands in the Minor Arcana.

When we add the swords of the knights who sought the Grail, we need only a disk to complete the four suits. In the Grail stories, a knight comes to a "wasteland" where he finds a wounded and unconscious king. While the knight watches, a group of women walk in procession up to the king, carrying the Grail and its attendant relics. They carry it on a disk, and so we get the Minor Arcana.

In some very early 15th-century Tarots, the Ace of Cups shows a lance upright in a cup or chalice, with a dove descending to the chalice with a wafer. The lance and the cup clearly signify the spear and the Grail, while a medieval legend claimed that on Good Friday the Holy Spirit, in the form of a dove, descended to the world with a consecrated host and placed it inside the Grail.

The Grail stories may predate Christianity, with the Grail cup a descendant of the Cauldron of the Goddess, ever-flowing with food. In the early part of the century, Jesse L. Weston's book *From Ritual To Romance,* described the Grail stories as the remnants of ancient rituals of initiation. She called the Tarot a record of those rituals in symbolic form. While the Minor Arcana represent the Grail relics, the Major Arcana reveal the steps of the initiation. There are, in fact, a number of direct Tarot images in at least some versions

The legend of the Holy Grail is the inspiration for one myth concerning the origin of the Tarot.

The Tarot Knight of Cups recalls the knights of Camelot on their quest for the Holy Grail.

of the Grail legend. The mother of the Grail knight, Perceval, dresses him as a fool when he ventures into the world because she fears his innocence and naiveté will put him in danger. He carries the qualities of the Fool card as well as his image. And in one version a Lord of the Moors dies hanging upside down, like the Hanged Man, the card in the Tarot that precedes Death.

Poet T. S. Eliot's famous epic work *The Waste Land* (1922) drew on the ideas described in Jesse Weston's book. Eliot even included a Tarot reader in his poem, the colorful Gypsy-like Madame Sosostris, "the wisest woman in Europe, with a wicked pack of cards."

Several modern Tarot decks have gone back to the Grail stories for their imagery. The Haindl Tarot pictures the Fool as Sir Parsifal, who loses his perfect innocence when he kills a swan. He must travel the symbolic path of the 21 cards to absolve himself. For the artist, Hermann Haindl, Parsifal's sin symbolizes the European destruction of the environment and indigenous peoples. The Arthurian Tarot, designed by Caitlín Matthews and painted by Miranda Gray, displays the Grail myths and their Celtic roots more directly.

The Haindl Tarot, Parsifal's killing
of a swan, symbolizes
environmental destruction.

The Fool

IV ARTHUR

The Arthurian Tarot gives life to
the many characters and story
lines of the Grail legend.

The historical record tells us very little about the precise origins of the cards. No one even knows the true origin of the word "tarot." Antoine Court de Gébelin claimed that it came from an Egyptian phrase *ta rho*, meaning "the royal road." Many people still believe this story, despite the lack of evidence.

historical knowledge

6

Other people have played with the sound of the word in similar ways. Unfortunately for all these theories, "tarot" is not the original name for the cards, but only a French shortening of the Italian name *tarocchi*.

There is a Taro River in northern Italy, not far from the area of the first known decks. Tarot publisher and historian Stuart Kaplan points out there is also a village called Taro in Burma, and that there is a Lake Tarok Tso in Tibet (in Austria *tarocchi* became known as *tarock*).

The Tarot (or *tarocchi*) first appeared, as far as we know, in the 15th century and almost immediately became popular and widespread. The first known deck, or fragment of a deck (only 67 of an 86-card deck, eight cards larger than the Tarot we know today, have come down to us), dates from around 1441, and the court of Filippo Maria Visconti, Duke of Milan. A more complete deck, with only four cards missing, shows up in 1450 as a wedding present for a marriage between the same Visconti family and a family called Sforza.

The two decks probably originate from the same artist, most likely a man named Bonifacio Bembo, who received several more Visconti Tarot commissions.

The 15th-century Cary-Yale Visconti Tarot. 74 of the original 78 cards of the Visconti-Sforza Tarot survive from the 15th century.

Early French 16th-century cards still reveal early Islamic influences, such as the use of coins as suit emblems.

Both decks display no numbers or titles on the cards. However, separate documents describe *tarocchi* with the same structure (22 trumps and 56 suit cards) as modern Tarot decks. Did the cards originate and develop their final form in such a short time? We might wonder how the nobility of the Visconti court played a brand new game without any numbers on the trumps to show their rank. Perhaps they simply knew which cards triumphed over which, the way we all know that a King beats a Queen in poker or bridge. If so, they would have had to memorize the order of 22 separate pictures, in a game that had just recently been invented. Or maybe they just kept a list alongside each player.

The Bembo cards in both decks are elegant, detailed – and clearly allegorical. In the older Italian deck we even find the three "theological virtues" of Faith, Hope, and Charity alongside the more common figures of Strength, Justice, and Temperance.

Playing cards entered Europe in the second half of the 14th century, probably from the Islamic world. The Crusaders may have brought them back from Palestine. We also know of playing cards in India and China, though any resemblance to Tarot appears remote. Not so the Islamic cards, for their suit emblems of polo-sticks, cups, swords, and coins likely inspired the very close European designs.

As cards became popular, they swiftly attracted condemnation from the church, and even legal bans.

Many Tarotists have seen these attacks as evidence that
the Tarot contained secret heresies, even occult magical
techniques. And it is true that the spiritual esoteric system
developed over time does contain a kind of heresy, a very
subversive one, for they teach us that we can find truth and
salvation through our own efforts rather than the help of a
priesthood or church. It also is true that some of the early
attacks described cards as the work of the Devil, some
even as the "Devil's picturebook" meant to lure people into
sin. And yet, the evidence indicates that these "thunders,"
to use Barbara Walker's apt expression, attacked the cards
primarily as games. Card games are frivolous and distract
people from piety and devotion to duty. They also lead to
gambling. Many of the edicts against cards also ban board
games and dice. And some of them specifically exempt
Tarot and chess, two games associated with the nobility
rather than the lower classes.

The Church condemned those
who used cards, believing them
to be the Devil's work.

HISTORICALLY BASED THEORIES

One of the most influential theories of the Tarot's origin comes from historian Gertrude Moakley, whose book *The Tarot Cards* links the trumps to the floats, or 257 "triumphs," in grand parades held during the Renaissance. The modern tradition of Mardi Gras and Carnival, with its costumes, mystery, and broken rules comes from these *trionfii* held just before Lent. Remember that the character of the Fool resembles the King of the Fools chosen at similar festivals in the Middle Ages. In the *trionfii* a man dressed as a fool represented Lent itself, dancing through all the floats.

The Mantegna Tarot's graceful Renaissance art raises its moral and spiritual lessons to high sophistication.

Even more significant to Gertrude Moakley's theory, the word "trump" for the 22 Major Arcana cards probably comes from the Italian word *trionf* or "triumph." In the popular card game tarocchi, the trumps, or *trionfii*, literally triumph over the lesser suit cards of the Minor Arcana.

Two variations on Tarot images demonstrate the symbolic quality of the cards in their early days. The Tarocchi dei Mantegna (Tarot of Mantegna), a set of 50 "cards" (actually prints) from around 1470, just 20 years after the Visconti-Sforza Tarot, is both a game and a set of lessons in moral, artistic, spiritual, mythological, and even cosmic ideas. The name comes from the painter Andrea Mantegna, long thought (mistakenly) to be the creator of the deck. The 50 cards divide into five series that depict the "Conditions of Man," "Apollo and the Muses," "Liberal Arts," "Cosmic

Principles," and "the Firmaments of the Universe." The cards are lettered by group, E for the lowest, Conditions of Man, A for the highest, Firmaments of the Universe (compare the Tarot Major Arcana, which begin with the simple Fool and end with the World). Within each group the cards are ranked by number so that the entire deck can work as a game. If so, the game instructs on a very deep level.

The second variation on Tarot images actually comes much later than the first known decks. However, its roots go back as much as 2,000 years. This is the tradition of alchemy, which came to its full flower throughout Europe in the 17th century.

Alchemy describes physical processes intended to transform "base metals," such as lead, into gold. A close reading of these processes and their texts makes it clear that the alchemists also sought to transform themselves, to "burn off" their ordinary, flawed humanity and unite with the divine, and even to become immortal. As one way to express their symbolic truths the alchemists produced a large number of beautiful and mysterious works of art. Many of these alchemical prints greatly resemble the standard imagery of Tarot cards, so much so that at least four or five modern artists have produced "Alchemical Tarots," either through reproduction of 17th-century pictures, or by painting their own works based on alchemical designs.

In the Middle Ages the King of Fools gave life to the symbols of anarchy, releasing social tensions in carnivals.

Alchemical Tarots have been created using 17th-century images.

Did the 17th century alchemists use the pictures in the popular game of Tarot as a source for their symbolism? Or did they both draw on a common underground source for their symbolism? The 15th-century Visconti-Sforza card of the Hermit in fact depicts an alchemist at work in his laboratory.

The occult tradition of Tarot interpretation points out the importance of duality in the Major Arcana. The deck begins with the Magician and the Papess followed by the Empress and Emperor, two pairs of male and female. It is true that in many cultural traditions, including alchemy, male and female symbolize such basic qualities as light and dark, action and stillness, reason and intuition, spirit and matter. Unlike the ordinary person, who accepts that such things will always remain far apart and are not capable of unification, the occultist seeks to unite them within the self and so overcome the limitations of ordinary existence. Many alchemical prints of the 17th century portrayed the perfect being as a "crowned hermaphrodite." We find this same image represented in some Tarot decks, as the dancer on the World card.

The Hermaphroditic World dancer, like the Alchemical perfect being, celebrates the many wonders of existence.

THE WORLD   LE MONDE   EL MUNDO

Some of the Tarot images suggest a possible connection to underground heresies. From its very beginnings, the orthodox Church battled a heresy known as Gnosticism. The word "gnosis" means, in fact, "knowledge," and the Gnostic Christians believed that the world we know is an illusion, or a prison, designed to keep us from our divine reality. When we acquire the knowledge of our true selves we will cast off the illusion and liberate the pure spirit within us. These very concepts have become incorporated into the esoteric tradition of the Tarot itself.

heresies

7

Possibly, just possibly, the Gnostic traditions influenced the Tarot images from their very beginnings. Gnosticism began in biblical times but it continued all the way into the Middle Ages and the Renaissance.

In southern France and Italy, in the centuries that preceded the Renaissance period, the Church ordered the extermination of entire communities in order to stamp out a Gnostic sect known as the Cathars in Italy and the Albigensians in France.

The first person to suggest an Albigensian origin for the Tarot was none other than Arthur Edward Waite, who was the designer of the Rider Tarot. Curiously, Waite suggested this idea as a satire on the many outlandish Tarot origin theories. He said, in effect, "We've got so many wild ideas, why not the Albigensians?" As Robert O'Neill, author of *Tarot Symbolism*, points out, we can never be sure with Waite whether a joke is just a joke. The occultists of that time often concealed their true meaning behind disguises. And he might have put the idea flippantly only because he knew he had not properly researched it. Waite cites a scholar named Harold Bayley, whose article *A New Light Cast on the Renaissance* argued that the Renaissance actually began in France, with the Albigensians. Waite wrote that if Bayley had known the Tarot he might have identified

Baphomet, and the earlier figure of the Greek goat-god Pan, inspired the demon so often seen in the Tarot Devil.

Gnostic elements in the cards. Bayley himself went on to write that in the 13th century and later, the Cathars and Albigensians infiltrated the papermakers and printing guilds, the very people who would make the Tarot decks.

Related to the Gnostic theory, another theory suggests that it was not just anonymous knights who brought cards to Europe, but in fact the Knights Templar, a strange and secret order of warrior monks. Originally formed in 1118 to protect Christian pilgrims in Palestine, the Templars became wealthy, powerful, and – possibly – involved in occultism, magic, and Gnostic dualism. Pope Clement V, under pressure from King Philip IV of France (who feared the Templars' money and power) dissolved the order in 1311, long before the first known Tarot decks.

Still, they may have brought dualist or occult ideas to Europe. The popular image of the Devil in the Tarot, a goat-headed – and hermaphroditic – demon, derives partly from "Baphomet," an idol supposedly worshiped by the Knights Templar.

The female pope

One particular trump card suggests a more specific heresy. This is the Papess, or female pope (in modern decks the High Priestess). Throughout the late Middle Ages and into modern times (including at least two recent novels), a legend persisted that a woman once became pope. Known as Pope Joan, she disguised herself as a man when young and became a priest. Over time, she rose to bishop, then cardinal, and finally pope, taking the name of Johannes, or John. Those who consider this a true story maintain that after the pope's death, when the Church discovered the truth, it wiped out the historical record.

This probably never happened. However, the idea of a female pope returns us to the Gnostics, for, among their other differences with the orthodox Church, the Gnostic groups ordained women as priests. And, in the late 13th century, a woman named Guglielma of Bohemia established a sect known as the Guglielmites. Guglielma taught that Christ would return in the year 1300 and create a new world in which women would rule as popes. The Guglielmites even chose the first woman pope in preparation. When 1300 came the Church of Rome made clear its authority. They burned the new "pope" at the stake. The woman's name was Maria Visconti. 150 years later, an image of a "Papess" appears in the *tarocchi* cards commissioned by her descendants.

Whatever its source, the picture of a female pope challenges the all-male authority of the Catholic Church.

No historical evidence exists to back up the claim that Tarot cards derive from the tradition of Jewish mysticism known as Kabbalah (the word means "received doctrine" and implies an oral, or secret, tradition). And yet, the links appear so compelling that the connection between the two has become the main line of symbolic interpretation, as well as the basis for many of the meanings used by Tarot readers in divination.

kabbalah

Many Tarot readers do not actually know this. They learn the meanings from a book about Tarot without much thought or concern for where those meanings originated. Nevertheless, Kabbalah (or *Qabala*, the non-Jewish occult version) is where they come from.

After the biblical period, with its visions and prophecies, Jewish mysticism took shape out of a remarkable short work called the *Sefer Yetzirah*, or *"Book of Creation."* Written sometime between the 3rd and 6th centuries C.E., the anonymous author produced a vivid concise series of meditations on the Hebrew alphabet. The Hebrew alphabet contains 22 letters. As we have already seen, there are 22 trumps in the Major Arcana.

This flowering version of the Tree of Life contains the traditional sephiroth, but shows them in vibrant living form.

We move now hundreds of years forward in history, first to Provence, France at the end of the 12th century, and then to the great flowering of Jewish culture in Spain in the years before 1492, when King Ferdinand and Queen Isabella expelled the Jews and Muslims from Spain and Portugal. The concepts of Kabbalah began to crystallize in this period, especially with the publication in Spain of a great work called the *Zohar*, or *"Book of Splendor."*

In their meditations on creation, the Kabbalists added another idea, that God created the universe in stages.

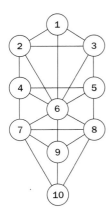

This geometric diagram for the Tree of Life loses the sense of a growing tree but allows us to see the 22 pathways that connect the 10 sephiroth.

There is not one world but four, the "highest" being a world of pure light closest to God, the lowest the world we know in our ordinary lives. The Tarot contains four suits, each with its own character. In each world, creation moved through a series of "emanations," which are known as *sephiroth* (the plural *of sephirah*).

Each world contains 10 of these sephiroth, each with its own unique quality. The names and qualities of the *sephiroth* remain the same in each of the four worlds – that is, *Kether,* or "Crown" exists as the highest *sephirah* in each world – only with a different energy determined by which world it is. The four suits of the Tarot deck each contain the same numbers, Ace through Ten.

Along with its meditations on the alphabet as a whole, Jewish mysticism has always focused on the four-letter name of God in the Bible. Known in English as the Tetragrammaton, these four letters *(Yod-Heh-Vav-Heh)* appear in the Bible without vowels so that no one can know their actual pronunciation. Ordinary Jews as well as Kabbalists consider this name as one of God's ultimate mysteries. We have already mentioned the four suits contained in the Tarot. As well as cards Ace–Ten, each suit contains four court cards, the Page, Knight, Queen, and King.

The *Zohar* and other early works focused primarily on the *sephiroth*. As an aid to their meditations they created various visual structures of the 10 emanations to show their relationship to each other. The most popular was a vertical structure known as the Tree of Life.

The Tree of Life became the means to unite the 10 *sephiroth* and the 22 letters (in Tarot terms the Minor and Major Arcanas). Kabbalists in generations after the Zohar speculated on 22 "pathways" between the *sephiroth,* one for each letter. There are many versions of these connections. However, the one illustrated on the opposite page is the structure best known to modern occultists and students of the Qabalistic Tarot.

Despite the fact that there are many variations of the Tree of Life itself, Tarot occultists have argued at great length as to the proper order of placing the cards on the 22 pathways. The numbers of the pathways are clear, but which card goes on which number? We might think of this as very simple – after all, the trumps are numbered as well, beginning with the Magician, card One, and ending with the World, card Twenty-two. But what of the Fool, number Zero? Do we place the Fool at the beginning? If we do place him in this position, then all the following numbers become misplaced. The place of the Fool has remained a problem for all those who seek a kind of Tarot orthodoxy.

And yet, this is exactly the Fool's special quality; his role is to upset applecarts, to make the Tarot impossible to pin down. The Fool brings the Tarot to life.

The basis of much Jewish mysticism is to be found in the Torah.

The Kabbalists considered the Hebrew letters living beings, older than the Universe itself.

How did the meditations of medieval Jewish mystics become linked to a game of 78 brightly painted cards sometimes used for telling fortunes?

the occult tradition

9

Some occultists will insist that the Kabbalist masters themselves secretly created the Tarot as a pictorial code for their abstract ideas. At the other extreme, some card historians strictly maintain that any connection between Tarot and Kabbalah is a modern fantasy. Possibly Kabbalistic ideas contributed to the cultural images that gave rise to the cards' allegorical pictures. And yet, it is difficult just to dismiss all those correspondences, in particular the 22 trumps and the 22 letters.

A facsimile from Court de Gébelin's *Le Monde Primitif*. The image is the same as the Tarot card Temperance.

The first suggestion of a link between the Hebrew alphabet and Tarot comes from Antoine Court de Gébelin, the same man who suggested that the Tarot originated in Ancient Egypt. Court de Gébelin was a Protestant pastor and a Freemason. In the 1770s he published a multivolume work entitled *Le Monde Primitif*, "The Primitive World." Today, such a book title would suggest a content based around the early stages of humanity. For Court de Gébelin, however, it called forth an ancient time of great wisdom. Volume VIII, published in 1781, contains his famous essay on the Tarot, with its claim that the cards form a disguised version of the Egyptian book of all knowledge, the famous *Book of Thoth*.

At one point in his essay, Court de Gébelin comments that the 22 trumps correspond to the 22 "letters of the Egyptian alphabet common to the Hebrews and the Orientals." Neither the Egyptians nor the "Orientals" have any such alphabet, however, the Jewish people do. Comte de Mellet, author of a further essay in *Le Monde Primitif*, introduced the method of linking the order of the trumps with the order of the Hebrew letters.

Almost all of Court de Gébelin's massive work has disappeared from our cultural history. Only his assertions about the Tarot cards have taken hold, gaining a life of their own. In their time they sparked a surge of Tarot fortune-telling in France. However divination through cards did not originate with the assertions made in *Le Monde Primitif*. There was already a flowering of interest in France. But the idea of the game of "Les Tarots" as a secret Egyptian book of mysteries and magic fascinated the public, and soon people began to apply the Tarot extensively to divination.

A grain salesman and print dealer (and some say wigmaker) named Jean-Baptiste Aliette reversed his last name to the more mysterious Etteila and created the

"Grand Etteila Tarots Egyptiens." There is very little of Egypt in Etteila's pictures, but they do evoke mystery and even wonder, with a level of art superior to many later occult Tarot decks. The deck was a great success. More than one version of it still exists today.

Unlike later decks, with their focus on symbolic systems, Etteila designed his cards for divination. They include images for male and female questioners, "Le Questionnant" and "La Questionnante" (both also bear the title "Etteila"). Each card contains a specific meaning, such as "This card announces the arrival of a relative from the country who has it in his power to do a lot of good" (from the booklet for the Grand Etteila deck, for card 22, "the King of France").

Etteila's deck, and his success as a professional fortune-teller, sparked a whole series of fortune-telling decks. Some of them had very simple designs, and labels like

These cards from the Grand Etteila Tarot depict the precise meanings in grand painterly style.

"a letter" or "Discovery." Others were more elegant, with scenes set in drawing rooms, or even mythological allegories, such as those in the "Grand Lenormand" cards, named for a famous cartomancer from the Napoleonic period. A certain Mlle. Lenormand, who claimed to be the confidante of Napoleon's wife Josephine, supposedly predicted the rise and fall of the emperor himself. Many of these decks (or modern reproductions) are still in print today.

ELIPHAS LÉVI AND THE GOLDEN DAWN

Antoine Court de Gébelin mentioned both the Tarot and the Hebrew alphabet only as an aside. The Kabbalistic connection might have never taken hold if it had not been for another remarkable Frenchman, a former seminarian and occasional political radical, Alphonse Louis Constant. Constant dedicated his work so deeply to Kabbalah that he took a Hebrew name, Eliphas Lévi.

Lévi sought to unite all the different strains of Western magic and occult philosophy. He went back to the time of the Renaissance and earlier, he used Egyptian ideas and images as well as Hebrew. He taught that we cannot really understand the Tarot without the Kabbalah, but also that we cannot understand the Kabbalah without the Tarot. Both, he thought, went back to the earliest human inspiration and inspired all the great works of humanity.

Eliphas Lévi set the Tarot into a coherent Kabbalistic system. That system reached its fullest development, and its most complex applications, with a secret group of ritual magicians who became known as the Hermetic Order of the Golden Dawn.

Founded in 1888 by a small number of Freemasons and Rosicrucians, the Order of the Golden Dawn lasted only 15 years. Its influence, however, continues to be felt to this day.

Dr. Wynn Westcott, founder of the Order of the Golden Dawn.

From its very beginnings, the Hermetic Order of the Golden Dawn wrapped itself in secrecy and deliberate legend. Members took an oath that if they should publicly reveal its teachings they would call on the spirit world to strike them down. The oath stated in part "… I submit myself, by my own consent, to a Stream of Power … as I bow my head under the Sword of the Hierus …" at which point the administrator of the oath placed the flat of a sword on the nape of the candidate's neck.

Partly this secrecy protected the members from persecution. Even today, people still fear the very word "occult" (which simply means "hidden"), and mistakenly assume it has something to do with black magic or the worship of the Devil.

Eliphas Lévi studied the links between the Tarot and the Kabbalah.

But there was another reason why the Golden Dawn concealed its teachings. The Order maintained that someone who studied its doctrines, worked its rituals, traveled the psychic pathways described by the Tarot, would reach a state of divine enlightenment – and on the way acquire great power. Secrecy was supposed to protect the secrets themselves from misuse, and protect as well those individuals who had not properly prepared themselves to receive the force that lived within the rituals, symbols, and magic formulas.

The Order of the Golden Dawn was started by three members of an occult group called the *Societas*

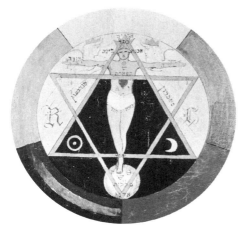

Rosicruciana in East Anglia, in the east of England: Dr. William R. Woodman, Dr. Wynn Westcott, and MacGregor Mathers.

Mathers claimed to find a "cypher manuscript," which, once it had gone through a process of decoding, led them to a mysterious "Fräulein Anna Sprengel" in Nuremberg, Germany. The three supposedly began a correspondence with her in which she gave them secret information and finally gave them the authority to set up a "lodge" in England.

2 THE HIGH PRIESTESS

5 THE HIEROPHANT

15 THE DEVIL

Cards from the Golden Dawn Tarot, a modern rendering of the deck that first systematized the Tarot's symbolic wisdom.

Contemporary people who have studied this story now believe that the cypher manuscript was a forgery, and claim that Fräulein Anna Sprengel is an invention.

This was not really unusual, however. Virtually every Masonic, Rosicrucian, or other occult lodge claimed some connection with ancient masters as evidence of their truth and authority. However, Woodman, Westcott, and Mathers carefully developed their material, putting together an astonishing system of rituals, philosophy, magical incantations, and correspondences between rites and symbols.

Artists and the Golden Dawn

The Golden Dawn included poets, artists, revolutionaries, and scientists. Its most famous member, the poet William Butler Yeats, stated much later in life that all his work derived from his study and practice of magic.

The members also included Moina Bergson Mathers, artist and sister of the philosopher Henri Bergson, theatrical producer Annie Horniman, and Irish activist, and confidante of Yeats, Maud Gonne.

The presence of the women in the Order was one of its most revolutionary aspects, for Freemason and Rosicrucian lodges had always restricted themselves to men. If we consider the significance of women in 20th century Tarot we can see what that single change set in motion.

The poet W.B. Yeats was a member of the Golden Dawn.

The Golden Dawn was unusual in opening its magical rites and ideas to women, such as Irish activist Maud Gonne.

THE GOLDEN DAWN TAROT

The Golden Dawn generated a huge system of ideas, symbols, and, in particular, rituals. It was not primarily an intellectual movement but a method designed to raise a person to a level of divine knowledge and power. And yet, just with Court de Gébelin and Lévi, both of whom wrote many volumes, what remains primarily of the Golden Dawn is the work they did in one particular area – the Tarot.

Like Lévi, the Golden Dawn considered the Tarot vital to a true knowledge of Kabbalah. The Tarot, they taught, was the very essence of the Kabbalist way of knowing God. And like Lévi they considered their Tarot to be the only true version, with the changes they made not a revision but a restoration, as if they had discovered a long lost "original" Tarot.

Initiates were expected to create their own Golden Dawn deck.

The story of the deck's creation supports the myth of a divinely given "corrected" Tarot. Supposedly, MacGregor Mathers took a set of blank cards into a locked room, went into a trance, and emerged a short time later with a complete painted Tarot. Today, almost no one believes this story, including the Order's most ardent devotees. Most people assume that Mathers designed the images, and then his wife, Moina Bergson Mathers, painted them.

A number of different decks have been designed by men and painted by a woman. Though the Golden Dawn brought women into its temples it did not consider them on the same level as men. Supposedly, men were more in tune with higher knowledge and abstract truth, women more sensitive and intuitive.

Even today, Tarotists tend to identify a deck by its intellectual designer and not by the person who made the actual pictures. People call the Rider cards "Rider-Waite" rather than "Rider-Smith," the Thoth deck "the Crowley Tarot" rather than "the Harris Tarot" after the actual painter.

Since the Golden Dawn considered its deck the true Tarot they expected everyone to use this particular set of pictures. They did not publish it, however. Part of what made the Order work was its emphasis on direct experience. Initiates had to copy the deck, drawing and coloring it by hand – though without any changes. Early members copied Mathers' own originals. As the Order grew larger, and the original founders died or resigned, new members copied the decks of those who had come before. The recent published versions of the Golden Dawn Tarot are all copies of copies of copies.

The first Golden Dawn deck was not published and the decks we now use are all copies of copies. They vary from the "original" Golden Dawn *(top)* to the New Golden Dawn *(bottom)*.

Some of the Golden Dawn Tarot images differ very greatly from both the decks that came before it and even later ones inspired by the Order itself. Since no one actually

This is the Lovers card from the Marseilles Tarot.

The Golden Dawn Lovers card is inspired by Greek mythology.

The Lovers from the Universal Waite has a more biblical style.

published a Golden Dawn deck until the 1970s, many people assumed that such decks as the Rider incorporated Golden Dawn designs. In fact, Waite and Smith's pictures look very different from those of Mathers. A good example is the Lovers. The Marseilles deck shows a young man who apparently must choose between two women while Cupid prepares to shoot an arrow at him. The Waite deck portrays a mature, naked couple standing apart from each other, while an angel blesses them. The Golden Dawn version, however, shows a scene from Greek mythology. The hero Perseus rescues Andromeda from a dragon. The allegory takes some decoding. According to Wang in his *An Introduction to the Golden Dawn Tarot,* Perseus symbolizes "the liberating effects of illumination," the rock materialism, and the Dragon fear. Andromeda represents the person who seeks to follow the spiritual path.

The Golden Dawn decks moved the Minor Arcana closer to full representation by showing a symbolic image on each card. More importantly, perhaps, they developed a system to determine the meanings for each card, based primarily on the *sephiroth* on the Tree of Life and the "element" for each suit. This greatly aided divination, for they gave a structure to the seemingly random meanings of the 40 numbered suit cards. We should notice here that all those decks that bear a "subtitle" on the Minor cards (one or two words to express the card's basic theme) are following the Golden Dawn (though often via Crowley, who made a few changes).

The Minor Arcana cards of the Golden Dawn Tarot became more symbolic in design, developing a system of meaning that was aided by subtitles.

PROMINENT GOLDEN DAWN SUCCESSORS

Three Golden Dawn-influenced decks have become among the most important of our time. The first, of course, is the Rider-Waite. We have seen how this deck actually strayed quite far from its source, partly because Waite wanted to pursue his own ideas, especially in the Major cards. His designs include symbols taken directly from Freemasonry. He also needed to keep in mind the Golden Dawn's demands of secrecy. The Rider deck came out in 1910, only a few years after the Hermetic Order dissolved.

The second Golden Dawn disciple was Aleister Crowley. Crowley joined the Order and rose quickly in its ranks, only to leave and begin his own group. A legend has built up around Aleister Crowley, one that he himself worked to cultivate. The newspapers of his time delighted in titillating their readers with reports of him as a wicked man, a "black magician" dedicated to evil and perversity. He certainly believed in excess. He took as his motto "Do as thou wilt – that is the whole of the law," a marked departure from an earlier occult dictum, "Do as thou wilt and harm none." But, despite his theatrical reputation, he also was a serious esoteric scholar, teacher, and dedicated Kabbalist.

Aleister Crowley cultivated his reputation as a black magician.

When Crowley decided to design a deck, he approached Lady Frieda Harris to paint it. The relationship demonstrates the power of collaboration. James Wasserman, in a pamphlet published with a recent edition of the deck, writes, "Crowley wrote to her that, had it not been for her artistic genius, he would never have gotten so deeply involved in the seemingly interminable process of creating a new deck; she forced him, he wrote, to realize each card as an individual masterpiece." The union of these two strong personalities produced a deck as remarkable for its elegant images as for the complexity of its ideas. In the court cards in particular Lady Frieda Harris brought a vivid life to usually static pictures.

The work took years, blocked by lack of money, slowed by Harris's dedication to detail, and hindered by the chaos of World War II. The pictures appeared first as illustrations for Crowley's book on Tarot, *The Book of Thoth,* published in 1944 in an edition of only 200 copies. The name, taken from Antoine Court de Gébelin, shows Crowley's mixture of

Below left
The original painting by Lady Frieda Harris of the Two of Disks. In older Tarot decks the Two of Disks was often the artist's signature card, like the Ace of Spades in modern playing decks.

Below centre
The Art Deco style of Harris' Queen of Wands radiates the furious energy of the Queen of Fire.

Below right
In the Thoth Knight of Disks energy radiates from the shield.

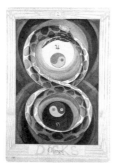

Queen of Wands

Knight of Disks

Yin and yang symbols from the Disks painting by Lady Frieda Harris.

homage to the past and sly humor. Both creators died before the deck was first published in 1969, Crowley in 1947, Lady Harris in 1962.

The third person to carry on the Golden Dawn tradition was a former vaudeville performer named Paul Foster Case. A wonderful story about how Case discovered the esoteric tradition illustrates the way a chance encounter – or maybe a guiding hand – can transform our lives. Case was standing backstage one day, waiting to perform, when someone else on the bill said to him, "Say Case, where do you suppose playing cards come from?" The question stuck with him, and he began to explore it – and discovered the Tarot, and through the Tarot, the esoteric world.

Case entered occultism too late to join the Hermetic Order itself. He did take part in one of its offshoots. He then went on to begin his own organization, The Builders of the Adytum (an adytum was the innermost sanctuary of a temple), known in the Tarot world as BOTA.

BOTA introduced something new to the occult Tarot. They went public. Unlike previous orders, with their emphasis on absolute secrecy, BOTA has always seen itself as teachers. They have made their materials available to anyone who seeks them, but in a cleverly controlled way. They offer a correspondence course. The lessons come one at a time, and the student may not move on to the next level until she or he has mastered the current one.

For the art, Case turned to Jesse Burns Parke, whose designs very closely follow Smith. The Golden Dawn required its members to hand-copy the deck and so make the Tarot their own. BOTA has found a simpler way to achieve this. The Parke cards come uncolored. As part of his or her training, the student must fill in the pictures according to a strict color scheme. In the BOTA world, all physical properties evoke precise psychic states, so that to use any but the assigned colors would damage the carefully calculated effect.

BOTA continues to this day. A great many Tarot teachers, card readers, and writers on the subject of Tarot symbolism have taken the BOTA course or have studied Case's remarkable writings.

QUEEN OF CUPS

The BOTA Queen of Cups follows the Rider version but with a greater emphasis on the symbolism of fish and water.

PART TWO

symbols and structures

When we look at Tarot cards for the first time, what we see in the main are beautiful and vivid pictures. Characters parade in strange costumes — they limp past a medieval church on a cold winter's night, they fall from crumbling towers in a lightning storm. Taken merely at face value, the cards fascinate us deeply. But, if each card simply showed an isolated moment in time, that fascination, wonderful though it is, might soon reach its limits. Instead, the cards continue to draw us ever deeper into fresh discoveries and wonders because the individual pictures form the surface of a living world. This is the world of structure and symbolism, a world where ideas and images move in and out of each other, giving birth to deeper awareness. Because of its symbolic structures, the Tarot can inspire us to marvel at the hidden beauties of the world. And, because of those structures, a Tarot reading can make a meaningful statement about our lives.

Twenty-two cards. Each with its special character, and yet, they all form a story, the journey of an innocent called the Fool. Virtually every version of the Fool card shows a character in motion. A tramp who tries to make his way along a road while a cat bites him. A young Egyptian trying to avoid a crocodile. In contrast to most of the people he meets in his journey, who seem to strike some kind of pose, the Fool is always moving, always going somewhere. But not just anywhere.

the major arcana sequence

10

The fool's adventures begin mysteriously, with a magician
and a high priestess, two guardians of secret mysteries.
From there they only get stranger, with hermits and
chariots, angels and devils, and even death himself. He
passes through darkness to ever brighter stages of light,
through starlight to the moon and at last the sun. And at
the end? The Fool, usually shown as a young man,
seemingly has changed his sex to become a beautiful
dancing woman!

The body of the Universal Waite
Fool suggests the Hebrew letter
Aleph.

Those people who see the trumps as a journey look for ways
to break the story into sections. One obvious way to do this
is to think of the trumps as two "acts." In the first act, our
lives build to their peak. We seek love and success. At a
certain point we sense, through changes in our bodies, that
life must move downward toward death. And so we look
inward and consider the meaning of things as we prepare to
leave the world for whatever transition death will bring.

There are two obvious cards to signal such a turn, and both
of them appear in the middle of the Major Arcana. The first,
the Wheel of Fortune card, represents the outward shift, the
way life reaches a high point and then begins to move
downward. The Hanged Man is the other card and it

THE FOOL.

The Fool always appears with an animal. In this Egipcios Kier version he tries to avoid a crocodile.

symbolizes the internal change as the person reverses consciousness from outward conquest to inward acceptance.

There is one problem with this view which is that Death comes immediately after the Hanged Man, with another eight cards to follow. This is a clear indication that Death does not signify the ultimate end or purpose of the Fool's journey. And applying such a story to the Fool does not really give weight to the cards' more mystical qualities.

Rather than seeing the Major Arcana in only two parts, we might consider it as divided into three acts. This division works very well when we set the Fool aside as the hero of the story, the character who must go through the experiences shown in the other cards. The Fool's number, Zero, also implies that we should consider it as separate from – coming before – the numbered sequence. With the Fool aside we get 21 cards, with a natural division into three groups of seven.

le Fou

A cat biting the Fool in the Wirth Tarot, based on the ideas of Eliphas Lévi.

The symbolism of numbers

The numbers three and seven figure very prominently in symbolism. We can think of Father, Son, and Holy ghost in Christianity; Brahma, Vishnu, and Shiva (Creator, Preserver, and Destroyer) in Hinduism; or freud's id, ego, and superego. The most powerful symbols come from nature. All of us come from a triad of mother, father, and child. The Moon goes through three stages – waxing, full, and waning.

The recurrence of seven in symbolic systems also comes from nature. The rainbow has seven distinct colors. In ancient times, people could see seven movable objects in the sky, compared to the more fixed background of the stars. These seven "planets" were the Sun, the Moon, Mercury, Venus, Mars, Jupiter, and Saturn. Around them, and their movements through the constellations, the ancient Babylonians constructed their astrological system which we still use, though in a modified form, today.

The Ancient Greek philosopher and mystic, Pythagoras, discovered that if you take a string that vibrates at a certain musical note, and keep dividing that string in half, you will get seven distinct notes before you suddenly return to the first note but at a higher level. These notes are the common musical scale, do, re, mi, fa, so, la, ti – and then back once more to do. This returning note is called the "octave" of the first.

Esotericists believe the seven notes in the musical scale carry special meaning and powers.

MOVING AMONG THE LEVELS OF THE MAJOR ARCANA

Now let us see how the importance of three and seven affect the Major Arcana. Suppose we look at the cards laid out in three rows of seven below the Fool.

Right away, we can see the idea of three levels of development – the conscious, the unconscious, and the higher consciousness. Each one begins with a dynamic image, the Magician in the first, Strength in the second (Justice in older decks), and that fearful Devil in the third. And each one ends with an equally strong image, the powerful Charioteer in the first line, the peaceful angel of Temperance in the second, and the World of the third.

Arranging the Major Arcana in three levels allows us to play with relationships between the cards. For instance, we can see "vertical" connections between cards in the same position. Justice comes below the Magician, and the Devil below Justice, so that we can call Justice the octave of the Magician, and the Devil the second octave. Look at the pictures in the Waite deck. Notice that the Magician has an infinity sign (a sideways 8) above his head, with an inverted pentagram (five-pointed star) above the Devil. Notice too that the Devil raises his arm in a gesture like the Magician's, except that where the Magician points his magic wand toward heaven, the Devil points his torch down at the ground.

The Fool

The Major Arcana from the Tarot de Marseilles. Following the practice of the Golden Dawn, Strength appears in position 8, and Justice in 11.

The Magician The High Priestess The Empress The Emperor The Hierophant The Lovers The Chariot

Strength The Hermit Wheel of Fortune Justice The Hanged Man Death Temperance

The Devil The Tower The Star The Moon The Sun Judgement The World

As well as the octaves, the numbers themselves suggest connections between the cards. There are two ways that higher numbers, 10–21, link to lower ones. The first connects the second digit in the higher number to a corresponding lower one. For example, the Devil is 15. The second number, 5, implies a link to the Pope (Hierophant). And when we place the two side by side, the Devil becomes a kind of parody of the Pope.

The second method of joining numbers is to add the two digits of the higher number and see what lower number results. The Devil is 15. 1 + 5 = 6, the Lovers. Once again, if we put the two cards together, we discover a resemblance. Adam and Eve in the Lovers become

Two kinds of power – the open creativity of the Magician, and the dark energy of the Devil.

THE MAGICIAN.

THE DEVIL .

Where the Hanged Man keeps his arms behind his back, as if holding his secrets, the World Dancer opens her arms wide.

transformed into the Devil's demons. Where the Lovers card symbolizes the fulfillment of mature sexual love, the Devil, with his chains around his subjects' necks, signifies unhealthy obsession.

Two other cards connect to each other in a special way, through their numbers and their images. 21 is 12 reversed. The picture of the Hanged Man, card 12, closely resembles the World Dancer, card 21, upside down. We can notice something else about the final card. The number 21 contains 2 and 1, the High Priestess and the Magician. The Dancer holds two magic wands, as if she has brought the opposites together in her dance of life.

The medieval Kabbalists believed that God created the world through 10 emanations of pure energy. They developed the symbol of the Tree of Life as a way to visualize the relations between those 10 sephiroth. Once they created this powerful diagram it became possible to experiment with it. Many of their visions have helped shape our understanding of the Tarot. One way the Kabbalists looked at the Tree was to see it as three triangles plus a final card. We might compare this to the three levels of the Major Arcana.

11

pathways on the tree of life

The top triangle, the one closest to God, represents the final cards, the realm of higher consciousness. The second triangle symbolizes the middle group of cards, the unconscious, and the third the conscious level (this is one of several possibilities). The final card, *Malkuth,* or "Kingdom," symbolizes the outer reality, but it also can represent the Fool who must journey through the challenges of three levels.

The Kabbalists also separated the Tree into three vertical columns. They called the right side the side of expansion, or mercy, and the left the side of contraction, or severity. If these two opposite columns existed alone, the universe would not survive, for they would pull so strongly at each other that they would tear it apart. The middle column creates a balance between the two. We find this theme in the Tarot. Many of the cards suggest a duality and a tension, often with some middle figure holding the two sides together. The angel blesses the man and woman in the Lovers, the Charioteer's strong will keeps together the black and white sphinxes, and so on.

One symbolic system connects the trumps to the *sephiroth* in a very specific way. Remember that the Hebrew alphabet

The Kabbalist, seen as a wise old magician. He grasps the final pathway on the Tree of Life that has taken shape from his meditations.

contains 22 letters, the same number as the trumps. The Kabbalists developed the idea of 22 "pathways" between the *sephiroth*. We have already seen the pattern. Here it is with the pathways marked for the cards.

We can use this diagram in several ways. One way is to understand each trump card in terms of the connection it makes between two particular *sephiroth*. The Fool belongs to the letter Aleph, the path that runs from the top *sephirah*, *Kether* (Crown), to the second, *Chokmah* (Wisdom). The crown signifies the opening to the infinite God. *Chokmah*, the same as that Greek idea of Gnosis, represents awareness of divine truth. We can look at the Fool's journey as the path between human understanding and the wonder of unknowable perfection.

The line between *Kether* and *Chokmah* does not go in one direction only. While we can imagine traveling "up" to *Kether* along this path, we also can think of the Fool leaving *Kether* and traveling "down" to the more human quality of *Chokmah*. This is why the Fool in the Waite card appears about to fall off a cliff, or why we sometimes describe the Fool as the soul taking on a body in order to become born and learn the lessons that can come only through a life in the world.

Individuals who work with the Major Arcana and the Tree of Life sometimes use the cards in specific meditations along the 22 pathways. The *sephiroth* and their connections are very abstract. The cards, on the other hand, present us with vibrant pictures, filled with action as well as symbolism. When we understand each card's place on the Tree, we can close our eyes and visualize the cards, and in this way move along the pathways.

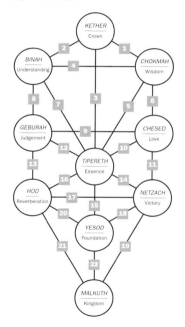

1 – THE FOOL
2 – THE MAGICIAN
3 – THE HIGH PRIESTESS
4 – THE EMPRESS
5 – THE EMPEROR
6 – THE HIEROPHANT
7 – THE LOVERS
8 – THE CHARIOT
9 – STRENGTH
10 – THE HERMIT
11 – THE WHEEL OF FORTUNE
12 – JUSTICE
13 – THE HANGED MAN
14 – DEATH
15 – TEMPERANCE
16 – THE DEVIL
17 – THE TOWER
18 – THE STAR
19 – THE MOON
20 – THE SUN
21 – JUDGEMENT
22 – THE WORLD

THE STRUCTURE OF THE MINOR ARCANA—THE FOUR TREES

The most direct connection between the Tree of Life and the Tarot comes in the Minor Arcana, with its Ace through Ten in each suit. Remember that the Kabbalists described four "worlds" and therefore four Trees. These Trees of Life correspond to the four suits of the Minor Arcana, with the special quality of each suit translating the special qualities of the numbers.

We will look at the numbers in two ways, first in terms of the *sephiroth,* and then in the tradition of numerology apart from the Kabbalist usage. The *sephiroth* with their Hebrew and English names and a brief description can be found in the box on page 93.

The sephiroth with their Hebrew and English names. Each suit "translates" the Tree into a particular kind of energy.

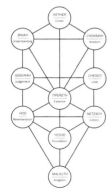

The Tree is a mystical vision, and the various *sephiroth,* with the possible exception of *Malkuth,* describe lofty principles. We may not always find the *sephiroth* practical for the ordinary use of the cards in divination. And yet, they give the Minor Arcana a special grandeur not so apparent from the pictures alone.

The *sephiroth* open the Minor cards to a world of marvels. If we wish to bring them more down to earth we can consider their numbers. From the beginning of human counting, people have seen great truths in the movement from one to two to three and on to 10.

The power of numbers is rooted in physical reality. We base
our number system on 10 because of our 10 fingers. The
first five numbers suggest aspects of the body, and the
world around us. We have one head, but two eyes, two
arms, two legs. One and two make three, the reproductive
number of mother, father, and child. Four signifies our four
arms and legs. It also joins us to the world through the four
directions, that is, in front, behind, and to right and left.
Five adds the head to the four limbs and so constructs the
whole person. If we stand with our legs apart and our arms
straight out to the side, we make the five-pointed star or
pentagram. This is the star that appears within the circle of
the suit of Pentacles.

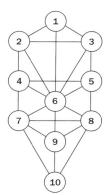

The five-pointed star links the human body to the heavens.
The ancients studied the movements of the planets
through the sky. Because we see the planets from our
earthly perspective we do not actually see the egg-shaped
path each takes around the Sun. Instead, we get more
complicated patterns, including loops, where the planets
seem to move backward for a time. We call these patterns
the "apparent motion." Over an eight-year period the
apparent motion of the planet Venus forms a pattern like a
five-petaled flower, or a five-pointed star. When we stand
with our arms and legs out we form the image of Venus.

The numbers six to 10 also suggest our physical reality,
only in more subtle ways. As the double of three, six
implies the generations. Seven and eight represent male

and female, for the male body contains seven openings (with the nose as one), and the female body eight. Nine reminds us of the nine months of pregnancy. And 10 of course represents the fingers that first allowed our ancestors to understand how to count.

Tarot writer Gail Fairfield has developed a number system based on geometry in the lower numbers and ideas in the higher. One represents a point, the simple emergence of existence. Two symbolizes the line that connects two points. With three we get a plane, or surface, for we have both length and width. Four allows solids to exist. The simplest geometric solid consists of four triangular sides. Five introduces time, with the possibility of loss. Six takes time to the next level, that of cycles and return. Seven brings in imagination and experiment. Eight returns us to reality, and nine interprets the different experiences. As the final number in the sequence, 10 both completes the pattern and forms a transition to a brand new beginning.

The pentagram, the most famous sign of magic, actually represents the human body.

Tree of sephiroth

KETHER – Crown. That which is above all else. Unity, perfection.

CHOKMAH – Wisdom. Intuitive awareness, truth.

BINAH – Understanding. The wisdom of the second sephirah becomes set into a context of experience.

CHESED – Love. The love that rules our lives when we act most in harmony with our emotions.

GEBURAH – Judgement. The ability to hold things back, to make hard decisions.

TIPHERETH – Beauty, also called Harmony. The center of the Tree, holding all the other qualities together.

NETZACH – Victory. Great strength and force of personality. Movement and grace.

HOD – Glory. The fulfillment of Netzach power, the ability to give form to that strength and grace.

YESOD – Foundation. At the bottom of the three triangles, Yesod reaches down into the unconscious. We can see it as the source of the images and symbols that make up mythology, the various worlds of meditation and astral travel, our dreams – and the Tarot itself.

MALKUTH – Kingdom. This sephirah links the three triangles to the outer world. Malkuth is the reality of physical existence.

If we take all these systems, and then compare them to the actual cards as they have evolved since Pamela Smith translated the Golden Dawn ideas into concrete scenes, we can construct a series of themes belonging to the Minor Arcana numbers.

the numbers on the cards

12

The Aces signify singularity. There is a purity in these cards, for they represent the basic quality of the suit, its "root" as the Order of the Golden Dawn described it. The Aces come to us as a gift from life, moments of special energy. The quality of that energy will depend on each particular suit.

Twos indicate duality, connections, dialogue. The various Twos deal with issues of communication and relationship. The Aces inspire, but the Twos act to develop and extend the original impulse.

When we go through the cards of the Tarot deck we will see that the character of a particular suit may work against the quality of the number. Cups symbolize love, while Swords represent conflict and tension. In the Waite image, the Two of Cups fulfills the number in the image of two people pledging themselves to each other. By contrast, however, the Two of Swords works against the number that it bears, with its picture of a woman who deliberately keeps everyone away from her. The central issue remains communication, but in this card we see its direct rejection.

Based on combining one and two, and the idea of the child, the Threes embody an early fulfillment of the suit. The

Though the Swords often represent conflict, the Ace here pierces through the world of the senses to abstract principles.

Imagine the woman dropping her Swords and taking off her blindfold to discover the love offered.

basic impulse of the Ace, developed in the Two, becomes established in the Three. Again, the suit changes the quality of the number. For Pentacles, this can mean mastery at work, for Swords it can mean heartbreak, for Wands success, for Cups harmony.

Four, the number of the first solid, symbolizes structure. We use the energy to build something, or dwell within a safe place, or hold on to what we have, or resist structure when it becomes confinement.

Despite the five-pointed form of the body, and its connections to the heavens, Fives show us loss and struggle. This comes partly from the idea that Five introduces time, with all its limitations, including sickness and death. We might say that, as the symbol of the body, Five brings us into physical reality, and so opens us to all the problems life can bring us.

The Sixes partake of the "beauty" and fullness of *Tiphereth,* the central *sephirah* on the Tree of Life. As the start of the second half of the numbers they allow a fresh beginning after the Fives. They also express issues of communication and the sharing of power and wealth. Inequality emerges in this number, with one person superior to others.

For the Sevens, we also look to the Kabbalistic image and find the theme of "Victory." We find both the masculine energy of the number and the theme that Gail Fairfield discerned, imagination. The person plays with possibilities and seeks victory over challenges through strength of will or through schemes and fantasies.

As the numbers approach the end, we see a theme of movement in the Eights, either toward consolidation or leaving what is already established. Eight is another number where the theme can conflict with the energy of the suit. Again, the clearest example comes with Swords. The suit represents trouble and conflict. When Swords come up against the idea of movement the result becomes obstacles, the way in which we can feel controlled by others and unable to move to free ourselves.

Nine is the last single digit number. It can represent a tension before the end. Something is established, but not without a price. The various cards show different compromises we make with life in order to create a place for ourselves in the world.

The Tens complete the suits. We see the most complete expression of the suits' qualities, for, like *Malkuth*, they establish us in the real world. However, not all the suits translate completion into happiness. For Wands, with their impulse to take on responsibilities and burdens, the Ten becomes oppressive. Swords show us the extreme of conflict. In Pentacles, the suit of money and physical reality, we get a sense of security and wealth, but somehow this is empty of emotion. Only in Cups do we find true joy apparent.

According to Tarot teachers Ruth Ann Brawler and Wald Amberstone the number of coils of rope binding the woman hint at secret Masonic initiation rituals.

ACE OF CUPS

3 CUPS 3

7 CUPS 7

The suit of Cups from One to Ten. These cards are from the Wheel of Change Tarot.

Now that we have seen how the numbers work through the pip cards in the suits, what of their regal companions? What qualities do the four Kings share, and the Queens, and the Knights and Pages?

the court cards

13

The Golden Dawn organized these cards in a clever way. As we shall see in a moment, the suits as a whole get their special qualities from what we call the four "elements": Fire, Water, Air, and Earth. We can understand these as a progression, with Fire as first and Earth as last. The Golden Dawn applied the same four elements to the four court card positions. As a result, each card became a combination of two elements. For example, Queens are Water, and so are Cups. Thus, the Queen of Cups becomes Water of Water. Swords, on the other hand, belong to Air, so that the Queen of Swords is Water of Air.

Unfortunately, these designations really only work with the Golden Dawn's altered cast of King, Queen, Prince, and Princess. For the conventional sequence, Page, Knight, Queen, and King, it makes sense to look at them as a progression based on the social position of the four characters. Pages are young, they have no responsibility except to learn, to become skilled through immersing themselves in the energy of the suit. In readings, Pages can refer literally to children, or students. They also can signal a time of study, or a person who is entering a new stage in life.

Knights are figures of action. Young in character, they want to explore and test their skills. They may be romantic or

The King of Wands, or Fire of Fire.

The Queen of Cups, or Water of
Water.

The Prince of Swords, or Air of
Air.

courageous. At the same time, they bear a responsibility to help others, for that is what knights do. Such a figure works well in the more aggressive suits of Swords and Wands, but can develop trouble in the introverted Cups, or the stable Pentacles.

The Queens and Kings both represent maturity. The Queens embody the more feminine aspects of appreciation of life – connection to family, enjoyment of the world and its wonders. This does not make them passive. We only have to look at them to see their strength. It does make them more involved with the world around them and with relationships. The Kings, on the other hand, rule. As the final card in the sequence they bear responsibility for society. They must make decisions and take action.

Some people will find this structure sexist. And there is no doubt that the court cards (as well as other aspects of traditional Tarot symbolism) flow from an old-fashioned and traditional view of male and female roles. We can go beyond this limitation if we recognize that the cards do not limit themselves in their applications to real people. In readings, a King may symbolize a woman if she shows the special traits of that card. And a man may act out the Queen of Wands, say, in the way he lives his life or in a particular situation.

We also need to recognize that these are not permanent designations. Unlike the Sun sign of astrology, which lasts a person's entire life, a court card in a Tarot reading says something about a person right now, not for all time. Think of them merely as characters in a play. The play does not last forever and the performers can change from one character to another while still remaining their essential selves.

Court cards and personality

People who do readings with Tarot cards often describe the court cards as the most difficult to interpret. They do not show an action or a situation or even an idea, but simply a character. Beyond the possibility of identifying actual people in our lives, how do we understand them? It may help to experiment with them in our minds. Look at the individual pictures. Try to characterize the differences between the four Knights, or the four Pages. Then think of your various friends and relatives.

Which one might fit the King of Swords, which one the Knight of Cups? Or think of characters in stories, and movies. What literary figure might represent the Page of Cups, with his dreamy stare into his chalice? Which of your favorite actresses would you cast as the Queen of Pentacles?

The Princess of Pentacles, or Earth of Earth.

The position of the card in the suit, its number, or place in the court, forms only half of the meaning for any Minor Arcana card. The other half comes from the suit itself. Theoretically, when we know the symbolism of the number and the energy of the suit, we can work out the meaning of any Minor Arcana card, with or without a picture.

the suits and their elements

14

Tarotists understand the suits primarily through nature images known as the elements. In the Middle Ages and earlier, people believed that all existence came from four basic states, Fire, Water, Air, and Earth. In modern time, science has discovered how to reduce matter to much more basic building blocks, such as electrons or neutrons. However, these ancient symbols still work, especially as a way to understand such things as attitudes to life.

As this waterfall reminds us, the element of Water is not always soft or gentle.

We can translate the four elements into modern scientific terms if we think of Water, Air, and Earth as the three states of matter – liquid, gas, and solid, with the element Fire as chemical interaction.

The liquid state, Water, evokes flowing emotion, changeability, imagination, and love. Air, the gaseous state, represents the mind, for we cannot see or feel our thoughts any more than we can see or feel the air that is around us. Like the wind, the mind shifts constantly; it is sometimes mild, sometimes stormy. The solid state, Earth, sums up whatever is real and physical, those things that we can touch or own, the ground we farm for food, our professions, and the money we receive for our labor. And the chemical interaction, Fire, symbolizes activity and movement.

Untamed, Fire can destroy. Controlled, it creates and transforms.

As always, Tarotists debate just which suits belong to which elements. Should Wands go with Earth because sticks grow in the ground? Or should Swords or Coins symbolize Fire, since we need flame to make each of them? As with so many issues, the majority of Tarotists follow the Golden Dawn, who saw Wands as Fire for their quality of action, Cups as Water, Swords as Air because a sword cuts through the air and symbolically pierces illusions, and Pentacles/Coins as Earth because that element embodies the material world, and so includes money and the magic of nature.

One way to understand the elements and the suits is to describe them as a process of creation. Fire begins it with the spark of inspiration. Water "receives" the initial impulse or desire – we contemplate what we want to do and we fantasize about the possibilities. Air, the mental element, plans and develops the project further. Earth, the element of physical activity, represents the finished project.

We can apply this structure to many things, from painting a picture, to making dinner, to developing a new product at the workplace, to becoming pregnant and giving birth to a child.

The suits

Wands

Here is a summary of the four suits. Wands symbolize action, adventure, optimism, energy, beginnings, and combativeness. Cups represent emotion, love, fantasy, passivity, and relationships. Swords bring us mental activity, conflict, pain, and aggressiveness. Pentacles evoke work, steadiness, security, money, nature, and responsibility.

Cups

These qualities do not exist in isolation from each other. We need to combine them in life, just as we see them combined in readings, in order to accomplish anything. Too much Wands' Fire will burn itself out, starting one thing after another without the determination to finish any of them. Too much Cups' Water will feel life so intensely that the person never does anything.

Similarly, Swords alone will lead someone to think constantly and ponder all sides but avoid action – the famous problem of William Shakespeare's Prince Hamlet. And Earth Pentacles alone will get caught up in endless detail, or lack the energy to change anything.

Swords

The suits weave in and out of each other in interesting ways. Wands and Swords are the masculine suits, both by their phallic emblems and their qualities of action, mental activity, and aggressiveness. Cups and Pentacles belong to such feminine qualities as love, relationships, home, stillness, and nature. At the same time, Wands and Cups suits tend to evoke a lighter, more optimistic tone, with Swords and Pentacles taking on the darker qualities of conflict and struggle.

Pentacles

Cups and Swords together represent the emotions, while Wands and Pentacles take us into the outer world.

More people know astrology than any other divinatory system, and they often wonder whether Tarot and astrology work together. Through the years, people have discovered different ways to do just that.

tarot and astrology

The basic method is to assign astrological meanings to the individual cards. When these cards come up in a reading, the reader can understand them partly in terms of their astrological symbolism. For example, if we connect the Magician to the planet Mercury (Mercury was the Roman god of magic), we can discuss the card in terms of what we know about Mercury. Or we might look at the importance of Mercury in the person's chart. You can also use this system to understand astrology better – if you understand the Tarot card of the Magician, this will help you grasp the concepts and mythological meanings around Mercury.

The qualities the ancient peoples observed in the planets still inform our astrological interpretation of them.

We are able to do this kind of interpretation with combinations of cards as well. Most systems link some cards to signs and others to planets. If the Magician appears with the Emperor, Aries, then we can think of the two as similar to what happens when Mercury enters Aries, or the reader might want to look at the person's chart and see how the sun sign and planet relate to each other.

Astrological attributions for the cards can help us with one of the most difficult parts of Tarot – determining the time when something is likely to happen. Readings often show a certain development that is likely to occur, but not when. We can look for clues within the reading. If the Magician and the Emperor appear, we might say that the change will occur when Mercury next enters Aries. As Mercury is a fast-moving planet, this would not take long. However, if Judgement came up, that would be Pluto entering Aries, a much longer wait.

Tarotist Carol Herzer has developed a system based not on planets and signs but on aspects. One card indicates a trine, another a square, and so on.

The most common system comes originally from the Hermetic Order of the Golden Dawn, though because of later modifications we might describe it as post-Golden Dawn. During the time of the Order, people knew only the seven planets of the ancients – the Sun, Moon, Mercury, Venus, Mars, Jupiter, and Saturn. These seven, plus the 12

Right
Aleister Crowley took the Golden Dawn astrological Tarot system and developed it to a high degree in the Thoth Tarot illustrated here.

Fool/Uranus

Justice/Libra

Magician/Mercury

Hanged Man/
Neptune

The Priestess/
Moon

Death/Scorpio

Empress/Venus

Temperance/
Sagittarius

Emperor/Aries

Devil/Capricorn

Hierophant/Taurus

Tower/Mars

Lovers/Gemini

Star/Aquarius

Chariot/Cancer

Strength/Leo

Moon/Pisces

Sun/Sun

Hermit/Virgo

Judgement/Pluto

Wheel of Fortune/
Jupiter

The Universe/
Saturn

signs, make 19. In order to match the 22 cards, the Golden Dawn assigned three cards the elements of Fire, Water, and Air, with the rationale that the Earth stands at the center of the whole system. But a few years after the Order ended, astronomers discovered three more planets. Suddenly, astrology and the Major Arcana became a perfect fit – 22 cards equal 12 signs and 10 planets.

Zolar's Astrological Tarot has a set of 32 astrological fortune-telling cards on the reverse of its Tarot pack.

ASTROLOGY AND THE MINOR ARCANA

With so many extra cards, the Minor Arcana allow us to get even more precise about the links to astrology.

The way we do this involves further arithmetic. There are 40 numbered suit cards. Of these 40, the Aces in each suit carry a special meaning. Whereas the other nine cards represent specific experiences, the Aces signify the element itself. Thus we can set aside the Aces to leave 36 cards. The astrological zodiac is pictured as a circle, and like any circle it contains 360 degrees. 36 cards gives us 10 degrees for each card.

There are 12 signs. They are not random but belong to the same four elements as the suits, with three signs for each

Below left
Known to the Greeks as Hermes, Mercury is the fleet-footed messenger of the Roman gods.

Below
Identified with Aphrodite, Venus is both the Purifier and the goddess of Love.

element. Nine (for the nine cards in each suit without the Ace) is three times three. In other words, each sign gets three cards. A. T. Mann, who was the creator of the Mandala Astrological Tarot, assigns a planet to each card. For example, the suit of Wands belongs to Fire. The three Fire signs are Aries, Leo, and Sagittarius. Aries gets cards Two through Four, Leo Five through Seven, Sagittarius Eight through Nine. But each sign also gets the planets of Sun, Mars, and Jupiter, arranged in different orders.

Finally, we come to the court cards. Once again, we need to play with the numbers. This time we set aside the Pages with the idea that they represent the element brought into the real world. This leaves 12 cards, the same number as the signs of the zodiac. Again we can divide these by element, with the three Fire signs going to the Wands King, Queen, and Knight, the three Water signs to Cups, the Air signs to Swords, and the Earth signs to Pentacles. Astrologers divide the signs of each element into three

In the Astro Tarot, each suit is assigned an element and a psychological attribute.

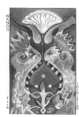

These cards from the Elemental Tarot use playful imagery to bring out the qualities of the court characters.

Astrological elements in the court cards

This gives us the following:

PENTACLES
EARTH

PAGE	element of Earth
KNIGHT	Virgo (mutable Earth)
QUEEN	Capricorn (cardinal Earth)
KING	Taurus (fixed Earth)

CUPS
WATER

PAGE	element of Water
KNIGHT	Pisces (mutable Water)
QUEEN	Cancer (cardinal Water)
KING	Scorpio (fixed Water)

SWORDS
AIR

PAGE	element of Air
KNIGHT	Gemini (mutable Air)
QUEEN	Libra (cardinal Air)
KING	Aquarius (fixed Air)

WANDS
FIRE

PAGE	element of Fire
KNIGHT	Sagittarius (mutable Fire)
QUEEN	Aries (cardinal Fire)
KING	Leo (fixed Fire)

types – fixed, cardinal, and mutable. The Kings set on their thrones embody the fixed signs, the Queens the cardinal, the Knights on their horses the mutable.

We do not need to memorize all these connections to work with the Tarot. In fact, we do not really need to use astrology at all to read Tarot cards. For those who do have some knowledge of astrology, however, the combination of the two systems can greatly increase our understanding of the meanings revealed in a Tarot reading.

Astrological elements in the pip cards

Here is the listing for each card:

PENTACLES

ACE	element of Earth
TWO	Saturn in Capricorn
THREE	Venus in Capricorn
FOUR	Mercury in Capricorn
FIVE	Venus in Taurus
SIX	Mercury in Taurus
SEVEN	Saturn in Taurus
EIGHT	Mercury in Virgo
NINE	Saturn in Virgo
TEN	Venus in Virgo

SWORDS

ACE	element of Air
TWO	Venus in Libra
THREE	Uranus in Libra
FOUR	Mercury in Libra
FIVE	Uranus in Aquarius
SIX	Mercury in Aquarius
SEVEN	Venus in Aquarius
EIGHT	Mercury in Gemini
NINE	Venus in Gemini
TEN	Uranus in Gemini

CUPS

ACE	element of Water
TWO	Moon in Cancer
THREE	Pluto in Cancer
FOUR	Neptune in Cancer
FIVE	Pluto in Scorpio
SIX	Neptune in Scorpio
SEVEN	Moon in Scorpio
EIGHT	Neptune in Pisces
NINE	Moon in Pisces
TEN	Pluto in Pisces

WANDS

ACE	element of Fire
TWO	Mars in Aries
THREE	Sun in Aries
FOUR	Jupiter in Aries
FIVE	Sun in Leo
SIX	Jupiter in Leo
SEVEN	Mars in Leo
EIGHT	Jupiter in Sagittarius
NINE	Mars in Sagittarius
TEN	Sun in Sagittarius

The traditional Tarot de Marseilles contains two angels, one on Temperance, and one on Judgement. The Waite deck and its successors add a third angel, replacing Cupid in the Lovers. They are all archangels, those mighty captains of the heavenly host. Their names all end in "el" the ancient Hebrew word for "God." Cupid is himself a kind of angel. Most modern versions of Cupid portray him as a chubby babe with little wings. But if we think of his Greek form, Eros, the God of Love, we can recognize his power. Eros — Love — overwhelms us and takes away our attempt to control our lives rationally. Like the figure of Cupid, angels have diminished over the years. Originally, angels were figures of great power, even terror in their awesome majesty. The huge wings in the Rider Temperance are so strong they cannot fit into the frame of the picture.

the world of symbols

The angel in the Lovers is Raphael, dedicated to higher intelligence. He belongs to the element of Air. The Hebrew name Raphael means "God heals."

The angel for Temperance is Michael, who in Christian mythology commanded God's army in the battle that defeated Lucifer and flung him down into Hell to become Satan. Michael is the archangel of Fire, ruler of the Sun. Temperance, the virtue of restraint, does not mean weakness, or boredom, but rather a powerful force for life.

On Judgement we find Gabriel, the most clearly identifiable archangel, with his trumpet summoning the dead to rise up from their coffins. Gabriel rules the element of Water. In Judgement we rise up from the deepest levels of experience. The trumpet call transforms and uplifts us.

Like angels, mythological beings in the Tarot all carry specific meanings.

When Hermes placed his winged staff, or caduceus, between two fighting snakes, they twined around it in peace.

hercules and the lion

Early cards of Strength showed a scene from Greek myth, Hercules slaying the mighty "Nemean" lion. For the Renaissance, the hero and his mighty club demonstrated fortitude. Later decks changed the scene to a woman gently closing the lion's mouth.

The Angelic Tarot brings the characters of Christian mythology vividly to life.

This term refers to a staff with two snakes wound around it. The Greek god Hermes (in Rome, Mercury) created this powerful object as a tool for peace and healing. It then passed to Aesculapius, a man whom the Greeks considered the founder of medicine. Doctors still use the image as a symbol of their profession.

Sphinxes symbolize life's riddles and dangers. They appear on the Chariot and the Wheel of Fortune cards.

Hades, Lord of the Dead, kidnaped the goddess Persephone and carried her underground to become his bride. Persephone's mother Demeter made the whole world barren until Zeus forced Hades to return her daughter. However, before the goddess Persephone returned, she ate two pomegranate seeds from Hades. As a result, she must spend part of each year underground as Queen of the Dead.

Demeter, the "grain mother," is suggested by the plants that surround the empress' throne, while Aphrodite (Venus), goddess of love, is suggested by the female symbol. Together the two goddesses evoke the twin passions of motherhood and sexuality.

the high priestess

We find Persephone in the High Priestess, at least in those decks that show pomegranates. The Star maiden also suggests Persephone, for the name means "She Who Shines in the Dark." Following Court de Gébelin, Tarot designers began to include Egyptian imagery. The Papess dropped her Catholic robes and reappeared as the High Priestess of the goddess Isis, sometimes as the goddess herself.

justitia

The figure on the card of Justice, with her sword and scales, comes from the same Roman goddess who appears over the doors of courthouses. However, the Tarot version is not blindfolded.

the wheel of fortune

Originally the turning wheel invoked destiny and the changes brought by time and the cycles of the year. Later, Egyptian imagery entered. In the Waite version and others, the snake going down on the left side is Set, the Egyptian God of death and destruction. The jackal-headed figure rising upward on the right is Anubis, guide to dead souls, and so a symbol of rebirth. The four winged figures in the corners derive from those four "fixed" signs of Babylonian mythology. They also signify the four apostles who wrote the Gospels. We see them holding books on the card, a medieval iconographic tradition.

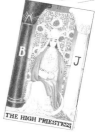

The pomegranates that surround the High Priestess link her to the "Greater Mysteries" of the Goddess Persephone, a nine-day ritual celebrated in Greece. The Empress suggests Aphrodite and Demeter, sex and the mother instinct.

Many of the most powerful symbols emerge from nature. Plants and animals possess a simplicity of purpose that strikes us humans, with all our complexity and struggle, as pure and meaningful. Over the centuries, nature has become part of that code of symbols, so that virtually every flower, every creature, in the Tarot does not exist solely as decoration but rather as a carrier of ideas.

the tarot garden

We have seen how the pomegranate brings forth
Persephone, who represents mysteries of life and death,
while ripe fields of grain (or a single sheaf) evoke
Persephone's mother, Demeter, goddess of fertility,
prosperity, and growth. The pomegranate also represents
the fertile potential of a maiden entering womanhood. The
red juice of the fruit signifies menstruation. According to
Fara Shaw Kelsey, a clinical herbalist, the pomegranate
contains "phyto-estrogens," plant chemicals whose
structure resembles the female sex hormone, estrogen.

People give roses to show love,
but also to ask for forgiveness.

Trees represent life itself, for they grow old and
strong, outlasting many human lifetimes. In many
cultures, people have worshiped trees as the
embodiment of the goddess. Some trees shed their
leaves in winter and seem to die, only to
return to life with the Sun in Spring, while
other trees remain green through the
darkest months and snows. Because of
their many branches, trees can symbolize
the evolution of experience and awareness.

Trees in the Tarot may evoke the Kabbalistic Tree diagram,
and ultimately the two trees in the Garden of Eden, Life and
Knowledge. The Gnostics, who may have influenced the

The High Priestess is linked with the peony in the Herbal Tarot.

Tarot's origin, turned the biblical story around. They argued that Eve led Adam to true knowledge (Gnosis) when she gave him the apple, and that our ultimate destiny is to join ourselves to the Tree of Life. We also can mention that in prebiblical times the goddess dwelt in her perfect garden (with her companion the snake) and gave her apple of immortality to those who passed her tests. In the Waite Lovers, the angel does not condemn Adam and Eve but blesses them instead.

Apples themselves carry special meaning. If you slice an apple in half horizontally instead of vertically you will find a perfect five-pointed star in each half. As we have seen, this pentagram evokes the planet (and goddess) Venus. This is why Eve gives an apple and not some other fruit to Adam, and why Aphrodite and other goddesses were often shown holding an apple.

Specific flowers carry special meanings. Most people recognize roses as symbols of love, for we give roses to each other to proclaim romance, or to ask forgiveness for a hurt. In the Tarot, roses mean desire. A red rose signifies passion, a white purity. Wild roses have five petals, a connection once more to Venus, one reason for the flower's association with the goddess of love, who lay in the original "bed of roses."

Sunflowers symbolize solar energy. Since they turn to follow the Sun's light, they indicate a love of life and its energy.

The BOTA Sun card shows four flowers in bloom, for the Kabbalistic four worlds of creation, with a fifth flower in bud, for unknown possibilities.

Lilies, sometimes seen with roses, have six petals and a cross-section like a six-pointed star. Most people think of this star as the Jewish "Star of David," but this is a modern usage from the 19th century. Its much older meaning invokes the union of male and female energy, for the upward pointing triangle symbolizes Fire, the primal masculine element, and the lower Water, the primal feminine.

The apple contains a five-pointed star, a suggestion of the body and the planet of Venus.

Some Tarot decks include the Asian plant, the lotus. The simple, exquisite lotus flower represents perfection and peaceful contemplation of the wonders of creation. It evokes the open yoni, that is the divine vagina of the goddess. "The jewel in the lotus" describes the union of male and female, for the jewel symbolizes the phallus (called lingam) of the God.

Recently, Tarotists have extended the use of plant symbolism. Writer Mary K. Greer has developed ways to use aromatherapy to draw out the powers and meaning of specific cards, while the Herbal Tarot links every card with a particular plant.

A sphinx or a jackal-headed man clearly symbolize an idea. In the Tarot world, so do ordinary animals. In the Middle Ages, artists produced wondrous books detailing the precise meanings of such creatures as the lion (a symbol for Christ), or the serpent (Satan). Many of these traditions found their way into Tarot images, joined in later years by images from Egypt and India and other cultures, as well as from esoteric doctrines such as alchemy.

snakes

There is something about snakes that both fascinates and repels us. The swift way they slither, their phallic shape joined to a feminine sinuousness, all these things stir deep emotions in people. Snakes represent primal unconscious energy. Snakes are poisonous, and yet the venom of some snakes (especially members of the cobra family) can produce ecstatic visions. Thus snakes serve to signify wisdom.

The Christian tradition describes the serpent as an incarnation of Satan himself. But that is only part of the whole story. The Gnostics describe the serpent as the secret hero of the Adam and Eve story. On the Mediterranean island of Crete 3,000 years ago, the goddess appeared holding snakes, or with snakes wound around her arms.

In order to grow, snakes have to shed their skins at regular intervals. This makes them a symbol of rebirth, or immortality. Moreover, a snake with its tail in its mouth represents eternity. We see this image as the belt on the Waite Magician's robe, and sometimes in an infinity loop around the Two of Coins or Pentacles.

Birds appear the very opposite of snakes. Where snakes disappear into the dirt, birds fly up to the heavens. Where snakes hiss, birds sing. Just as snakes symbolize the

Odin, with the ravens Thought and Memory in the background, acts out the Hanged Man sacrifice as he reaches down for the prophetic Runes.

Father of Cups in the North
King of Cups

unconscious, so birds represent the higher consciousness. Snakes are sexuality, birds spiritual awakening. And yet the two are connected, as shown in dragons and feathered serpents. When unconscious energy rises up from the base of the spine to the top of the head it becomes transformed into the flash of enlightenment. In India, people call this energy kundalini and picture it, unaroused, as a coiled serpent at the base of the spine. When it rises up to the third eye and the crown it bursts forth as a bird. In myths and some Tarot pictures we see the Tree of Life with a serpent at its roots and a bird in the topmost branches. The lightning flash in the Tower can be described as the kundalini released.

birds

In alchemy and ceremonial magic, the lion embodies passion.

Birds symbolize truth, art (for their songs), and prophecy. Decks that draw on Norse mythology (for example, the Norse Tarot and the Haindl Tarot) will show two ravens, the messengers of Odin. Their names are Thought and Memory. Owls signify wisdom and the quest for knowledge. The trained falcon on the wrist of the woman in the Nine of Pentacles represents the disciplined mind. Also in the Waite, and the BOTA, a small bird appears on the Star. This is an ibis, messenger of the Egyptian gods, and sacred to Thoth, legendary creator of the Tarot itself.

The other common creature of the air is the butterfly. Because they begin life as sluglike caterpillars and then seem to die in coffinlike cocoons, only to emerge into beauty and flight, butterflies signify transformation.

the fish

A fish signifies the soul. It swims through the river of emotions and the great sea of the unconscious. The fish is the emblem of Cups/Water, along with the porpoise, who unites intelligence to instinct. Wands (Fire) animals are the lion and the salamander, said to live in fire. Pentacles (Earth) display such creatures as the rabbit, symbol of fertility.

the lion, king of beasts

The lion represents noble character, but also passion, especially in Strength, where the developed mind tames the wild energy.

the goat

Goats, seen mostly on the Devil, signify lust and sensual appetites.

The goat's ability to eat a great variety of foods makes it a symbol for indiscriminate desire.

Moon's half-light stirs our deepest instincts.

the fool

He almost always appears with an animal, a dog, cat, or a crocodile, at his heels. They represent the animal side of our nature, seen as benign in the Waite image, where innocence reigns. In older decks they are perceived as a force that bites and drives us until we learn to overcome it. Animal instincts emerge most powerfully under the influence of the Moon, where we see a dog or a wolf, but no people. The other creature on that card, the crayfish or crab or lobster, symbolizes the deepest level of instinct, a nameless feeling we can never fully comprehend.

18 THE MOON

To the esotericist, the whole world, from the grand patterns of the constellations and planets to the lines in a person's hand, becomes a picturebook of symbols. Three kinds of creation may signify the three levels of awareness. Aspects of the landscape represent the unconscious, or animal instinct. Buildings and other human creations represent the conscious mind and its ability to transform nature. And the great figures of the sky symbolize the higher consciousness of eternal truths.

as above, so below

19

These symbols do not stay within tight boxes. Mountains rise up from the dirt to penetrate the sky, and so they represent the quest for truth and the mind's ability to grasp abstract ideas. Similarly, towers reach up toward the heavens and so indicate human aspiration. But if they become closed, so that we cannot see the world outside, then they become a prison of pride and illusion.

Lightning destroys the Tower of illusion. Do we experience this as disaster or liberation?

In comparison to the solidity of mountains, water symbolizes formless experience – emotion, dissolution of the ego, release, and cleansing. These things have a sexual meaning as well. While the Earth as a whole is thought of as female, for it gives birth to all life, the shape of mountains suggests the phallus, Water is traditionally feminine, while Fire is masculine.

Rainbows combine water and light to create beauty. In the Bible rainbows represent God's mercy, while in Norse mythology the "Rainbow Bridge" joined Earth to the world of the Gods.

Through all these nature symbols we must find our way. Paths in the world of the Tarot indicate development or pursuit of wisdom. Sometimes they lead from the waters of the unconscious to the mountains of knowledge.

Sometimes, as in the Fool, there is no path, only the courageous leap into new experience.

The final seven cards of the Major Arcana move from darkness to light. They begin with the Devil and his oppression. Then, in the Tower, lightning strikes as the flash of truth destroys the gray prison. The released soul now must journey back to the World, the literal title of the last card. To do so, it passes through stages of light. The Star symbolizes perfection, yet the realm of this card lies far from ordinary human experience. The Fool journeys through the Moon, the borderland of dream and myth. When the Moon appears in other cards we know that we are dealing with emotional states, intuitive wisdom, and mystery. Then comes the Sun, symbol of reason, clarity, awareness. Judgement, the penultimate card, shows the Fool transformed, liberated to a knowledge of the angels.

The Moon, reflective and intuitive, illuminates the mountains of knowledge.

Human constructions and artefacts symbolize aspects of experience. A house represents the self, the varied rooms the many parts of our lives. If the house expands into a castle, it may indicate security and wealth, but also someone bound in by possessions and responsibility. A canopy shows us open to nature and exploration. A canopy of stars symbolizes our connection to the heavens, and the way cosmic patterns affect our lives.

Beyond the personal psychology of the self, buildings can symbolize the structure of the universe. And when we see a key we know that we are ready to unlock something, whether it is our own psyches or the secrets of existence.

Occultists have traditionally called the Major Arcana keys, each one a means to unlock some special truth.

The B and J on the Universal Waite High Priestess card stand for Boaz and Jakin, the names of the pillars on the entrance to Solomon's temple in Jerusalem.

Pillars

One human structure deserves special mention. This is the pair of columns that appears on many cards, especially the High Priestess, the Hierophant, and Justice. They derive from ancient images, in particular the two columns at the entrance to Solomon's temple in Jerusalem. The columns symbolize duality and the fundamental pairs of existence, such as light and dark, male and female, action and stillness.

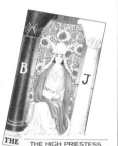

Often we see a curtain strung between the two pillars. These too come from ancient times, when people believed that God dwelt in the innermost part of the temple, where no one might enter. Even today, in synagogues, a curtain covers the Ark that contains the Torah (the five books of Moses). The Tarot curtain also evokes Isis, who was said to wear a veil to hide the glory of her divine face. The curtain or veil has come to symbolize the separation we experience from the secrets of creation. To know the wonders beyond the veil is the goal of esoteric work.

PART THREE

the cards

And so we come to the cards themselves. We have looked at the vast number of decks and variations between them, and the complex history of symbolism, and yet, after all the analysis and origins, the images remain. An old saying describes a picture as worth a thousand words. We might think of a Tarot picture as worth a thousand pages, for as Tarot books increase each year we approach that quantity of commentary. And the pictures still tantalize us.

Just why does the Hanged Man hang upside down, and why by one foot? What exactly is that Tower that has been broken open by lightning? Is it the Tower of Babel? What do the women in the Three of Cups celebrate so joyously? A Moon ritual? The birth of a child? Why does the Queen of Swords look so grim as she sits on her throne? Does she know sorrow, anger? Or a dedication to truth? Such questions, and many more, continue to haunt us no matter how many years we spend in study. And they should, for this is how we truly come to know the Tarot and its wonders, through returning again and again to the cards themselves.

Whether a beautiful boy about to leap off a cliff or a tramp wandering through the world, our Fool enters into the miraculous journey of the soul like a newborn child. He — or she, for the Fool represents the quest of women too — will face life's challenges, and must learn to make something of himself.

the journey of the major arcana

20

The fool begins with two primary encounters. Seen one way, the Magician represents an actual person who has studied and trained himself to gain control of the hidden forces of nature and the invisible world. The High Priestess shows someone who has delved deeply into all the hidden mysteries of creation. Seen another way the Magician and High Priestess embody basic principles of existence: light and dark, action and stillness, male and female. The Fool cannot master these things, because he is only a Fool, after all. For now, he must go on to the specifics of life.

Full of enthusiasm, the Fool begins the adventure into the Tarot.

0 — THE FOOL

Children see their parents as all-powerful, the center of a confusing universe. Mommy and Daddy, goddess and god – the Empress and the Emperor. One nurtures and gives life and food and love, the other teaches and disciplines and creates structure. (These qualities do not mean that actual parents act according to this strict division. In reality, every parent partakes of both principles, the Empress in some moments, the Emperor in others.) As well as the family drama, the two cards symbolize nature, the Empress through the abundance of life, the Emperor in the scientific and spiritual laws that underpin all existence.

As the Fool grows he must learn the traditions of society. The Hierophant represents education, especially religious, for the Tarot leads us to spiritual wonder. But we can learn and study all our lives and never understand without direct experience of life. The first thing that pushes us into such experience is love. Through our sexuality we discover ourselves, beyond the beliefs of our parents and the doctrines of our teachers and priests. And so the Fool grows up. He takes charge of his life, he drives the Chariot of his personality to victory over life's challenges. The world looks at him and sees a success. But he is still a Fool. And so he wonders – he knows the world, but does he know himself? He sets out on a new journey, a psychic one.

He will need Strength for such a journey. He might unleash some inner lion. But the Fool trusts life, and its joys, and therefore Strength comes naturally. The Fool withdraws for a while, looks inward. He explores hidden things in therapy, or else studies the esoteric discoveries of those who have gone before. He shines a light on his own psyche. And a kind of vision emerges – life as a great wheel of change. The Fool sees events, as well as actions. He glimpses the mysteries that shape a life.

The Magician gives the Fool a glimpse of life's possibilities.

From the Empress the Fool learns abundance, passion, warmth, and love.

As the Fool matures, he takes control of the Chariot and meets life's challenges.

What will he do with such knowledge? Will he deny it and hide? Or will he accept the Justice of who he is? We know the answer. He is a Fool, and Fools do not hesitate. They leap into truth the way they leap into experience.

Acceptance brings surrender, then sacrifice, but also a wondrous discovery. An eternal Tree of Life grows through all our individual lives. The Fool attaches himself to this Tree and discovers he can reverse his values. He can let go of the things that seemed so important to others. He can let them die. Through the death of these old parts of himself the Fool discovers angelic power – and serenity.

Now he has conquered life's challenges, then given it all up to die and emerge as an angel. Only a Fool would give up such balance and perfection. Only a Fool would go down into the dark of existence in search of Devils. The Fool finds his Devil, his shadow forces. He goes into the dark Tower only to unleash the lightning of revelation.

He finds himself now in a world of beauty, among the Stars. But he knows he must make his way back. He travels through the mysteries of the Moon to the bright light of the Sun. Now the Fool gains wisdom. It is as though a trumpet summons his soul, for now the Fool understands, deep in himself, all the things that once appeared intellectual or symbolic. The Fool now dances lightly on one foot, arms out as if to embrace the World. Innocence has finally become wisdom.

The Fool cannot complete his journey without encountering the dark energy of the Devil.

The lightning of truth blasts away whatever might have imprisoned the Fool.

At the end of the journey, the Fool dances, his arms embracing the World.

SETTING OUT

Zero. Nothing. No-thing. We are always unable to pin the Fool down. Whenever we think that we understand him completely, he dances away and laughs – not scornfully, but with joy. The Fool gives the Tarot life. Without him, the cards in the Tarot deck would become stiff figures in formal poses. The Fool strips away all our pretensions, especially those concerning knowledge and achievement. Do we think we understand the Magician, or the Star? Have we memorized all the symbols in the Tarot, delved into the cards in meditation? The Fool dances us away. Multiply any number by zero and you get – zero. Do we think we understand life? Ourselves? The Fool moves us on.

In the Golden Dawn tradition the Fool receives the letter Aleph. The rabbis tell a story about this letter. Over generations they debated among themselves what portion of the Ten Commandments God spoke directly to all the Israelites, and what portion only to Moses to inscribe on his tablets. At first they said God spoke the first three, the sacred commandments, to the people and the seven moral laws to Moses. Another generation said, no, God spoke only the first, the announcement of His presence, "I am the Lord, your God, who brought you out of bondage." And then a new generation said that God needed only the first word "I am," or in Hebrew *"Anokhi."* Finally came a rabbi who moved away from all fixed ideas,

The Golden Dawn gave the letter Aleph to the Fool, the letter that is silent, nothing.

for he said that God needed only the first letter, Aleph, for Israel to know Him. Only – Aleph is a silent letter. No sound. No-thing.

The Fool leads us to take risks, do something impulsive, wild. He calls to the child inside us, the part of us that wants to follow our instincts, to do something, without plans or careful analysis.

Is the Fool always right? When this card appears, look carefully at the other cards. What will happen if we obey our "Foolish urge?"

Reversed, the meanings can shift in at least two ways. Most simply, the card can advise caution. Look down before you step off a cliff. Or, it might say that we act recklessly, acts that may seem like instinct but in fact stem from escapism and fear.

Fool, Tarot de Marseilles. The cat symbolizes the impulses that move us on our journey.

THE FOOL

Above all else, look at the gesture. Very clear in the Rider, more subtle in the Marseilles, it shows the body as a channel for power. Artists and writers – like ritual magicians – know that the ego, the conscious self, does not really create anything. Instead, all our training and preparation serves to allow us to get out of the way. Something moves through us. Something that wants to be created. This is what it means to experience magic, to open yourself to the power of life.

Magician, Visconti-Sforza Tarot. This earliest known deck dates from the 15th century.

The wand draws down the energy from the "heavens," that is, the unknown sources of creation. He does not hold this energy in his body, for that would achieve nothing. Instead, he lets it move through him into reality. Think of the times energy has flooded you so that you cannot sit still, or you say to someone "I'm so excited I could just burst." If you do nothing, the feeling just passes – or becomes disturbing. But if you use the energy the power continues.

Consider a gardener. All his knowledge and skills amount to nothing if he does not actually make things grow. In the Waite deck the flowers at the Magician's feet symbolize manifestation. On his table we find the four suits of the Minor Arcana. His knowledge and skill have made him a master of the elements.

In a reading, the presence of the Magician announces a time of power and creativity in your life. Experience the joy of this time, but use it wisely and with ingenuity.

As card One the Magician signifies the beginnings of projects, especially original and creative work. Where the Fool indicates the leap into action, the Magician indicates the actual start. One, the archetypal male number, can indicate masculine sexual power, forceful and confident (like all the other cards in the deck, the Magician is not restricted to one gender).

The card also means will, as the mind and training focus on a goal.

As a reversed card, the Magician can mean that energy becomes blocked or disrupted. Projects fall apart, optimism drains away. The person finds it hard to focus. Nevertheless, the presence of the card states that the power is there, but that something is holding this power back or denying it.

Alternatively, the reversed Magician can signify a corrupt use of power.

Magician, Tarot de Marseilles. The items on the table resemble the Visconti-Sforza version.

The High Priestess wears a crown that originates from Isis, a goddess of Ancient Egypt.

TWO TAROT WOMEN

The Fool encounters this silent figure on his way from one powerful character to another, the masculine Magician, and the very feminine Empress. The High Priestess is not sexless, but she represents a particular feminine archetype, the withdrawn virgin. The Greeks portrayed some of their most powerful goddesses as virgins, in particular Athena and Artemis. Artemis (Roman Diana) was a Moon goddess, symbol of the new, or "maiden" Moon, and we see lunar images on many High Priestess cards, such as the crescent at the feet of the Waite version. Her Isis crown also signifies the Moon, now in all three phases, with the circle in the center as the full Moon, and the two horns the waxing and waning.

The High Priestess guards the veil of secrets, all the inner mysteries of life. Usually she holds a locked book or a rolled up scroll, symbol of the great truths hidden from us at this early stage in our journey. The High Priestess promises that such mysteries exist, and at some late time we too may understand them. We sometimes assume that the idea of veiled mysteries means that something is held back by secret masters – concealed information. But look carefully between the curtain and the pillars of the High Priestess. What lies behind is simply still water. The depths of the unconscious. The ego can only survive by pretending that we exist separate and isolated from the world around us. To lift the veil of consciousness of the High Priestess would "drown" us in the wonder of existence. We cannot accept this, but the High Priestess card allows us to gain a glimpse of it at the level of inner awareness.

In readings, the High Priestess stresses stillness and withdrawal. We need to spend time looking inside, contemplating, seeking peace more than answers. The card suggests that sense we sometimes get of a great truth we cannot put into words. Any attempt to explain would only destroy it. Thus, she symbolizes both intuition and silence.

Reversed, she emerges from her withdrawal. She becomes more emotional, passionate, more involved with others. She may reveal long-buried secrets.

Far left
Papess, Tarot de Marseilles, holding the book of life's mysteries.

Left
High Priestess, Universal Waite Tarot. Her rolled-up scroll symbolizes hidden truths.

This is a favorite card for many people. She is loved for her warmth, passion, her promise of abundance and prosperity. She embodies feminine power and devotion.

The Empress draws on several figures from mythology, including the grain goddess Demeter and Aphrodite/Venus, the goddess of love. Western culture has created an artificial split between women's sexuality and motherhood. A moment's thought will remind us of just how women become mothers. The Empress, therefore, signifies all great passion, and an approach to life that holds nothing back.

The "Great Mother Goddess" of mythology reaches beyond the immediate meaning of human birth to fertility for the world in general. From the earliest cave paintings, humans have associated growth and abundance with female sexual energy. Humanity's oldest images include symbolic versions of the vulva. And because she means fertility she means abundance in other areas as well – wealth, luck, nourishment of our bodies and our emotions, pleasure.

The grain goddess, Demeter, is one of several mythological figures upon which the Empress draws.

For both men and women, the Empress in a reading signifies a passionate approach to life, emotion, and sensation rather than thought. Like someone in love, or a mother devoted to her baby, the Empress gives herself entirely. She also promises abundance and "fertility," not just sexual, but creative fertility, even productive work. Look

carefully at the other cards, however. As with the Fool, the Empress' passion may not suit a situation. Emotions may ignore facts, as when we love someone who treats us badly. One very specific meaning – the Empress may represent an actual mother, either the querent's mother or the querent herself.

Reversed, she can indicate infertility, or even mother's rejection. Some more positive meanings suggest a movement away from passion to a more rational and thoughtful approach to the issues in the person's life.

Left
The Empress, Universal Waite Tarot. The river of emotion pours through this card.

Centre
The Empress, Motherpeace Tarot, celebrates several ancient goddesses.

Right
The Empress, Tarot de Marseilles. Some later decks interpret the chair behind her as wings.

TWO TAROT MEN

Just as many individuals respond warmly to the Empress' motherly love, so they often recoil from the Emperor's patriarchal discipline. They look at the Waite deck and see his stern face, his armor, the desert all around him. In contrast, a river rushed through the lush garden of the Empress. Other decks have tried to give the Emperor a more positive image. The BOTA and Alchemical show him as a spiritual ruler, more abstract and symbolic. The Haindl deck shows masculine vitality as a young ruler strides away from the World Tree.

The Emperor is often seen as a strict father, who sets necessary rules.

In the center of the first line of seven cards, the Emperor becomes a test. Passion and abundance nurture us, but we cannot grow unless we deal with the rules of society, the laws of nature, the ability to think rationally and plan for long-range goals. We dislike the Emperor the way we dislike all rules, going to work, or paying our taxes. But we need to accept such things if we want to become adults.

More widely, the Emperor signifies civilization itself. We may find him less joyous than the Empress, but without civilization we would spend all our energy struggling to stay warm and fed. And beyond the laws of humanity, the Emperor can symbolize the greater laws of existence, as revealed in science and metaphysics.

People dislike the Emperor because they see him as representative of society's rules. If they see themselves as the Emperor then he can become a symbol of their own power to define and defend their territory. Women often need to become their own Emperor.

In readings, the Emperor may indicate an actual father the way that the Empress can signify a mother. More usually, he signifies rules and structures. He reminds us of laws and the authority behind them. He also may represent a strong person who sets boundaries and is willing to defend them. Finally, the Emperor suggests the need to act responsibly.

The Emperor

The Emperor, Haindl Tarot. Here, the Emperor symbolizes the vitality of a young male.

Reversed, the Emperor loses his harshness and becomes more compassionate, and also more emotional. At the same time, he may have trouble with clear thoughts or decisive action.

The Hierophant (or Pope in the older Tarot decks) is the Emperor's partner more so than the Empress in many ways. Where the Emperor signifies laws and society, the Hierophant symbolizes education. He represents the traditions and knowledge that we need to learn to function in our culture. Most specifically, the Hierophant embodies the religious teachings of our heritage.

Hierophant, Thoth Tarot, painted by Lady Frieda Harris.

The Hierophant

In the Waite deck and others, we see the Hierophant with disciples at his feet (this is the first of the many cards that show three figures in a triangular relationship – see also the next two cards, the Lovers and the Chariot). These disciples look to him for guidance and instruction. Like the High Priestess, he sits between two pillars. The High Priestess, however, had no followers. She remains silent, a keeper of inexpressible and hidden mysteries.

The Hierophant (or High Priest) symbolizes the religious ideas we can express. He conveys the outer levels of religion, its doctrines, institutions, and moral codes. These things are all important. They give us an intellectual basis as well as a moral structure. And yet, the Hierophant's pillars are a uniform dull gray. The pillars of the High Priestess, with their lotuslike capstones, glow dark and light, symbols of vibrant energy. And the curtain that blocks the entrance to her temple hangs with lush pomegranates.

People often dislike the Hierophant the way they dislike the Emperor. They think of him as a repressive church and an artificial morality. Many now seek genuine spiritual experience outside religion. This is a new trend, and we do not really know what it will produce. In most human cultures, the mystics and others who sought direct knowledge of Spirit did so within their traditional religions. For instance, the Kabbalists were strict Jews, the Sufis devout Muslims.

In a reading, the Hierophant indicates teachings, especially religious traditions. It also can suggest orthodoxy and conformity. Individuals behave according to social conventions and restrictions. This sounds narrow, but it may give them a sense of belonging to something.

The Pope from the Marseilles Tarot blesses his disciples.

In relationships that concern marriage, the Hierophant represents institutions – the laws, rules, and the expectations of marriage rather than its emotion.

Reversed, this card becomes a symbol of unorthodoxy and those who seek their own path through life rather than follow the one that society has laid out for them. It may also indicate an excess of kindness, or draw attention to susceptibility, and gullibility.

LOVE AND TRIUMPH

The traditional version of this card shows a young man between two women, one dark-haired, the other blonde. Many see it as a choice between different paths in life, or at least between possible partners. Cupid readies his arrow. One of life's great lessons is the realization that some choices come from a deeper level than rational decision.

The Lovers, Universal Waite Tarot. The angel's blessing unites Adam and Eve.

Because the dark-haired woman often looks older than the blonde woman, some readers describe her as the young man's mother. Through sexual desire we break from our parents. And not just in matters of sexual relationships. Spurred by sexual energy, we start in adolescence to become our own person, with our own beliefs.

The famous Waite image shows the power of a mature relationship. The angel who blesses the man and woman symbolizes the way love raises each person to a higher level, so that the partnership becomes a whole far greater than the sum of its parts.

The three Waite figures also show aspects of the self, so that the card does not always mean a relationship. The man symbolizes conscious awareness, the woman the emotions and unconscious energy. The angel signifies that higher consciousness that we seek as we move through the trumps. We need knowledge and reason but they can take us only so far. The "royal road" to our higher consciousness travels through the unconscious.

The first meaning of the card in readings is always a relationship. Whether the relationship takes place now, was in the past or will be in the future, or whether the person simply desires a relationship, will reveal itself in the other cards.

With the older decks, the card signifies a choice, sometimes between two partners, but other kinds of choices as well (if the person has asked about, say, business, the meaning will shift). With the Waite and other modern decks the card symbolizes fulfillment.

Reversed, the card symbolizes something that goes wrong in a relationship. Jealousy may interfere, or different goals and interests may separate them. Sometimes the reversed Lovers can mean simply that the person cannot expect to find a partner at this moment in time. It also may mean difficulty making choices.

Top
The Lovers, Shining Woman Tarot. The divine and the human embrace each other, both in relationships and within the self.

Above
The Lovers, Tarot de Marseilles, shows a man about to choose between two women.

The Chariot, sometimes called Victory, culminates the first line. With his powerful presence, he signifies the person who has successfully traveled through the challenges of the previous cards. It seems our Fool has grown up.

The Chariot, Tarot de Marseilles. The charioteer holds a wand in his hand, similar to the Magician.

Most decks do not show the Chariot in motion. He has already journeyed to a place where he can take a firm position. At the same time, most decks show two animals, horses or sphinxes, one black and the other white. They symbolize the problems and contradictions in life. The charioteer has not really resolved all these troublesome issues. He holds his life together through confidence and force of personality.

What others see as success, and contentment, may in fact form a mask, something we project into the world and come to accept as our true selves. At such points – our times of triumph and confidence – we need the Fool to resurface and remind us that we are not our possessions or accomplishments.

The Charioteer represents will. At its best this does not mean control or grit-your-teeth-and-hang-on. Instead, the will focuses energy to a purpose. It unites the qualities and

lessons of the previous cards. The Charioteer
holds a wand like the Magician. He wears
lunar (High Priestess) symbols on his
shoulders. His canopy of stars recalls the
Empress. The square block suggests the
Emperor. The sphinxes kneel like the
Hierophant's disciples. We find the
Lovers subtly in the sexual "lingam and
yoni" symbol on the front of his Chariot.

In readings, the Chariot signifies a
strong will. The person will deal with a
difficult situation through force of
personality. However, this does not
mean aggression, but confidence
and a belief in potential solutions.
The situation may involve problems
or contradictions that the person
cannot easily resolve. Generally,
the Chariot indicates someone
successful, admired by society
and the people around him.

Reversed, the Charioteer's will proves too weak to keep the
problems from pulling the situation apart. This does not
have to mean disaster. Instead, it may liberate the person
from a stressful situation. A gentler interpretation simply
advises the person to let go of trying to control what
happens.

The Chariot, Universal Waite
Tarot. Following Eliphas Lévi,
sphinxes have replaced the
horses that we see on the
Marseilles version.

A FRESH START

Before the Golden Dawn, card Eight was Justice, and Strength Eleven. The Order switched the two for Kabbalist reasons, but we can see the value thematically. Strength acts as a counter to the Chariot. When the Fool gives up control she can discover her inner Strength. Now instead of a forceful personality, she uses gentle persuasion.

And Strength works well as the "octave" of the Magician. Like him she displays an infinity sign (her number Eight turned on its side) above her head. Both show a calm and firmness of purpose without aggression. The Fool needs Strength to give up the Chariot's outer success and turn inward toward self-discovery and surrender.

Strength reverses the gender of trump One above it. Feminine gentleness joins the Magician's openness to creative energy. Instead of a snake for a belt she wears a garland of flowers (though some decks change the lion – symbol of passion – to a serpent, symbol of kundalini sexual magic). The card also becomes more personal. The Magician appears remote, something we respect but cannot picture as ourselves. Strength's simplicity allows us to imagine ourselves there, holding the lion, unafraid.

Older decks show Hercules and his virtue of fortitude. Quite early, however, the card changed from violence to

Strength, Carey-Yale Visconti Tarot. The lion symbolizes strong emotions.

persuasion. But the lion does not have to mean enemies, or danger. It also symbolizes strong emotions or desires that may threaten to overwhelm. More broadly, the lion represents all the aspects of ourselves that we suppress or deny. The Hercules approach beats down those troubling qualities or desires and refuses to give in to them.

Strength indicates confidence and ease in readings. The person faces problems with hope and trust in her own ability to deal with whatever lion roars at her. In a crisis reading, Strength assures the person that she can do what needs to be done.

Reversed, Strength remains, but the person doubts herself. Her emotions may get the best of her, or she may believe she simply cannot face her problems – or herself.

Left
Strength, Thoth Tarot. Crowley's design urges us to experience our passions.

Centre
Strength, Universal Waite. The figure wears a flower garland to symbolize the creative power of love.

Right
Strength, Ukiyoë Tarot. The figure's expression suggests firmness of purpose.

Card Eight brought a female quality to the Magician position of the first card in the sequence. Card Nine now changes the female High Priestess to the male Hermit. Where the card above him stressed intuition, the Hermit brings in the masculine quality of study and analysis as he holds up his lantern of knowledge. And yet, we can see his connection to the High Priestess. His twilight setting recalls her deep blue background. Like her, he looks inward, withdrawing from involvement with others so that he can search for the hidden truths of life and the self.

A person may become a hermit to search for spiritual enlightenment.

In many times and places, people have literally become hermits to search for spiritual experience. Hermits live in the woods, or in caves, or in deserts. They go on temporary vision quests or they spend years in meditation. What joins them all is the need to separate from human culture and its outer directed goals – money, fame, relationships – in order to discover some greater truth. They enter dark physical space to seek an inner light. But they do not always remain apart. When they have found their vision, or revelation, they may return to help others. Thus, the card of the Hermit may signify a person in a time of self-examination, but it also may indicate a guide or teacher who can help the person.

Through trump Eight we found the Strength to begin a new journey. Card Nine shows the actual beginning. The person steps back from his normal life to probe the dark ignored parts of himself and his experience.

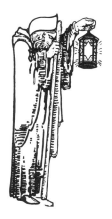

In readings, the Hermit card signifies a time to hold back from activities and personal involvements. The person needs to spend time alone and look at who he is. He may want to cut back on his social or work commitments. If you ask about a relationship and you get the Hermit, either for yourself or the other person, you know that this is not the right time. As a wise old man, the Hermit also may symbolize maturity.

Reversed, the Hermit card indicates a return to the world. Withdrawal will only isolate the person. The reversed card also may indicate a Peter Pan kind of person who refuses to grow up.

The Hermit, Cary-Yale Visconti Tarot.

The Hermit, Haindl Tarot. He withdraws from civilization but embraces all of nature.

The Hermit, Elemental Tarot. He has learned how to raise up primal energy.

SHAMAN 9

IN MY WEAKNESS DO NOT FORSAKE ME

DO NOT BE AFRAID OF MY POWER

WILL

VISION AND HONESTY

the wheel of fortune

Below the Empress we find the goddess Fortuna, goddess of luck but also of the turning year. The cycles of nature, especially the way the Sun fades and returns, and the way plants die and come back to life, all imply the idea of continual rebirth. Traditions that teach of reincarnation often describe the soul as moving from life to life on a turning wheel. Sometimes we rise up, sometimes down, according to laws we do not fully understand.

The term "Wheel of Fortune" reminds us of roulette and other gamblers' games. Our lives sometimes depend on events we cannot control. The Tarot itself is a game, sometimes played for money. As in readings, the game works because we cannot control where the cards will fall. The Wheel of Fortune card signifies our lack of control over the outer circumstances of our lives.

And yet, the Wheel also forms the Hermit's vision, his recollection of what has shaped him. According to Buddhist tradition, at the moment of enlightenment, the Buddha visualized and understood every moment of every lifetime, from the smallest insect to the loftiest god. Although we cannot expect such a mighty revelation ourselves, we can try to remember the ways the Wheel has turned for us in this current lifetime.

On the compass points of the Wheel we see the letters T-A-R-O. We can read these as ROTA – Latin for wheel, TARO – Tarot, ORAT – Latin for speaks, TORA – the Torah, or Hebrew law, and ATOR – an Egyptian goddess of life. ROTA TARO ORAT TORA ATOR – The Wheel of Tarot speaks the law of life.

The Wheel of Fortune is often a difficult card to interpret in readings. It tells of a turn of events that the person cannot control or even rationally predict. A man walks into a room and meets his great love. A person perfects an invention only to find that someone has patented the same idea a week before. Sometimes – but not always – the other cards will hint at what the Wheel change might mean. We cannot control the way the Wheel turns, but we can work on our own reactions.

Reversed, the card suggests that the person has trouble adapting to change. It does not necessarily predict bad fortune.

Right
Wheel of Fortune, Golden Dawn.
The Wheel turns in a mysterious light.

Far right
Wheel of Fortune, El Gran Tarot Esoterico. This card signifies our lack of control over many things in our lives.

This powerful card comes at the center of the Fool's journey. It forms the central test. Can we look honestly at ourselves and accept the truth of what we have done, what has happened to us, where the balance rests between our own actions and the circumstances given to us by life? If we can do this, we can move on to the higher levels. If we cannot summon the honesty required for this card we may remain stuck in resentment and denial. The card comes below the Emperor. The goddess Justitia replaces the law of society with the spiritual law of truth.

The number Eleven recalls the Magician, card One, and the High Priestess, Two (1 + 1). The imagery also blends the two extremes. Justitia (Themis in Greek) sits before a curtain like the Priestess. At the same time, she raises her sword like the Magician's wand. The sword points straight up as a symbol of commitment to honesty. Through Justice, and her balanced scales, we begin to combine genuinely what seemed absolute opposites.

In courts, the scales of Justice are often tilted, indicating that the court must decide for one side or the other.

Two very important symbols help define this card. The first is the scales. On courthouses, the scales of Justice are often tilted, since the courts must decide for one side or the other. Spiritual justice, however, requires that we understand the balance between the different sides of our experience. These include both what we have done and what others have done (especially in relationships). People who say "It's all my fault," as well as those who say "I'm just a victim" have not balanced the scales.

The eyes form the second symbol. The courthouse Justice wears a blindfold to symbolize the impartiality of the law. But spiritual Justice demands that we look honestly at our lives. Only through such honesty can we balance the past and the future and go forward in our lives.

In a reading about a court case, Justice signals a truly just outcome (this may not mean victory!). In personal or work conflicts it indicates fairness between the people. More widely, it calls for honesty with one's self. We need to assess our situation, work out where our part lies, and decide what comes next.

Reversed, the card warns of some injustice, either in a conflict or in our own behavior. We may need to look under the surface of some situation.

The Magician and High Priestess imagery combines in Justice from the Universal Waite Tarot.

Justice, Light and Shadow Tarot. In Tarot, Justice keeps her eyes open, and the scales balanced.

REVERSAL AND RELEASE

Tarotists differ on the interpretation of this card. For some it means being caught in some problem (hung up). Others see it as a necessary or painful sacrifice. Some even call it a betrayal, after the Italian custom of hanging traitors upside down. The coins that fall from his pocket in some decks may indicate a thief, or Judas Iscariot, who betrayed Jesus for 30 pieces of silver. However, the Visconti-Sforza (the oldest known deck) shows a young man perfectly at ease in his upside down position.

Hanged Man, Visconti-Sforza Tarot. This shows a man at ease in his reversed position.

The Fool began this stage of his journey by turning away from outer success. Now, after Justice, he can reverse the outer values of society. And so we see him upside down. His posture mimics the World dancer (12 is 21 backward). Without Justice, he might very well find such change a hard sacrifice. But if he has passed that test he understands that he can attach himself to something greater than his personal power. The branch he hangs from extends from the Tree of Life, that is, the spiritual source from which the Magician's power comes. Here the Fool understands spiritual support as something real. Coming below the Hierophant, he has found a greater connection than doctrine and rules.

The Hebrew letter for this card, *Mem*, means Seas, or Water. With trust in life, the Hanged Man can allow his rigid

The Hanged Man

Hanged Man, Haindl Tarot. The god Odin joyously gives himself to the Earth.

THE HANGED MAN

Hanged Man, Mythic Tarot, based on the story of Prometheus.

The Hanged Man 12

Hanged Man, Egypcios Kier Tarot.

attitude to dissolve into a oneness with life. Such openness prepares him to face the next card, Death, without fear.

In readings, the Hanged Man describes a reversal of previous attitudes. The card may say that the person already experiences the new outlook, or that such an approach would help in the current situation. More widely, it symbolizes a person who sees things differently from society or the people around him. He does not do this out of deliberate nonconformity, but because of attachment to a greater belief.

Reversed, the person loses that sense of attachment. He may become influenced by social pressure or the opinion of others. The card does not condemn him for this, but reminds him to look within himself for deeper values.

Hanged Man, Merlin Tarot derives from a Welsh tale of a "threefold death."

XIII HANGED MAN

This is the scary card, the one that always turns up in the movies, usually with murder soon to follow. No matter how many books on Tarot insist that the card does not mean anyone's death, people still recoil from the name and the sight of the skeleton.

The medieval allegorical image of Death harvesting bodies served to warn people against pride. No matter our state in society, we all must die. The picture may have its roots in the practice of "planting" dead animals as an offering to the Earth for fertility. In Tarot, Death has evolved into the concept of releasing aspects of ourselves that are old and worn-out. The Fool began this part of the journey with a search for a true self behind the mask. Through Justice he came to understand himself, and then the Hanged Man allowed the Fool to trust in life beyond the ego. Now he can let that outer mask die. None of this makes Death easy. We blithely call it death-of-the-old-self and ignore how traumatic many people find letting that old self die. People stay in bad marriages, or hopeless jobs, often for years, because they cannot let it die. The Tarot reminds us to trust in what will come afterward.

Death comes below the Lovers. In Shakespeare's time people referred to orgasm as "the little death." Both cards involve a release of the ego. In the Waite image we see four responses to Death. The king lies dead, the only one who is struck down. The bishop stands upright. The maiden

Top
Death, Jacques Vieveille Tarot. Death is shown as the Great Reaper, a reminder that we must all die, whatever our position in life.

Above
In the Death card from the Universal Waite Tarot, four responses to the ultimate end are recorded.

In the movie, "The Seventh Seal," the knight plays chess with death, symbolic of man's inability to cheat death.

symbolizes a state between innocence and fear. The child, however, greets Death openly. He has not yet built up a mask of self-protection.

The appearance of Death in a reading indicates some kind of change. Something needs to die so that the person can move on to a new experience. This might prove to be a very difficult period of transition, but the other cards can reassure them of the new possibilities that will come if they allow change to occur.

If Death is reversed, it indicates that something is stuck in a person's life. Waite describes this state as "inertia, sleep, lethargy," the outer, physical symptoms of resistance to change.

PREPARATION FOR DESCENT

Below the Chariot, at the end of the middle level, we see a different kind of triumph. Here the Fool has passed the various tests of an inner initiation, he has "died" and been released to a sense of life that is both peaceful and joyous.

The Temperate person does not need to go wild to know the wonders of the world.

People who have not found genuine serenity often confuse Temperance and find the idea repressed, the image boring. Ask a group of Tarot novices to choose their favorite pictures and not many of them will seize upon Temperance. As symbolic as it appears, we need to experience it to understand. But remember – this is the archangel Michael, leader of the heavenly army.

Temperance, Oswald Wirth Tarot. Note how the water pours at an angle.

The angel pours water from one cup to another, blending aspects of life. In the Oswald Wirth Tarot (Wirth was a disciple of Eliphas Lévi) one cup is gold, the other silver. He combines the solar and lunar qualities of the Magician and High Priestess. The Latin word *temperare* means "to combine properly." Notice that the water pours at an angle, a physical impossibility. To the intemperate person, the ability to respond serenely to life seems magical.

XIV — TEMPERANCE

Temperance, Morgan-Greer Tarot.
The triangle represents
spirituality.

The Haindl Tarot captures the
idea of blending: sun and moon,
gold and silver, death and life.

Alchemy

The angel stands with one foot in water – the emotions, and one foot on land – actions in the world. A path leads from the water to where the Sun rises between two mountains. If we look back at Death we will see a similar sunrise between two pillars. Life energy leads us beyond duality.

In readings, Temperance calls for a calm approach. The Temperate person avoids going to extremes, and instead finds a middle path in difficult situations. It may urge the person to do nothing, just stay calm in the midst of others' craziness.

Reversed, the person finds it hard to act in a moderate way and instead goes wild, often overreacting or getting caught up in other people's emotions. We can use the image of Temperance right side up in a meditative way to restore inner calm.

Temperance, Motherpeace Tarot. The African dancer is more dynamic than the usual figure of an angel.

After Death, the Devil appears most often in movie scenes. The monstrous figure, with his chained demons, reminds us of the Tarot's reputation as "black magic," even the work of Satan himself. In fact, one of the themes of the card is illusion, and there is no greater illusion than the idea that the Tarot controls us in some destructive way.

The goat-headed demon does not come from ancient images of Satan (a Hebrew term that simply means "adversary"), but rather Baphomet, the supposed idol of the Knights Templar. The picture also evokes the Greek god Pan. Pan was a god of excess, not evil, a god of wild abandon, whose panpipes supposedly drove people to wild frenzy, especially sexual. Some modern Tarot decks have changed trump Fifteen to Pan.

The Devil, Thoth Tarot. This card symbolizes the misuse of psychic and sexual power.

In the Waite deck, the Devil, Fifteen, seems a distortion of the Lovers, Six (1+5=6). In place of passion blessed by an angel we find demons chained to a stone block. Look closely, however, and you will see that the wide loops on the chains would allow the two just to lift them off and walk away. Illusion holds us, not actual slavery.

Why does the Devil start the last stage of the Fool's journey? Why does it follow Temperance? One answer reminds us that we need Temperance to confront our own Devils and not get caught in their illusory snares. The Fool achieved a personal transformation in the second level.

The journey now takes him to confrontation with universal forces. But he cannot seek the light of revelation, without a descent into darkness. We all carry Devils within us – fears, past traumas, dark desires. We cannot find complete freedom until we look at them honestly and know that they do not enslave us. We can walk away.

In readings, the Devil shows an oppressive situation, especially a bad relationship. It can mean sexual obsession, or some kind of addiction. It also can indicate anxiety – in other words, whatever chains us. We need to see that the real oppression is, in fact, illusion.

Reversed, the person begins to free himself. Sometimes this means walking away from, or resisting, an oppressive person or situation.

The Devil, Universal Waite. The goat-headed demon is modelled on Baphomet, alleged idol of the Knights Templar.

STORM AND RELEASE

The Tarot is optimistic. Life, it teaches, does not allow us to remain immersed in illusions or oppression. However, if we do not free ourselves the pressure will build up until something explodes. The stone tower of our pain crashes around us and we discover ourselves flung free. We may not enjoy this experience. But it will liberate us.

The Tower card evokes various tales. In the story of Rapunzel, the sorceress throws both Rapunzel and the prince from a tower without a door. In the modern fantasy *The Lord of the Rings,* the end of evil comes with the destruction of a "dark tower." And in the Biblical story of the Tower of Babel, God destroys human attempts to build a tower to heaven and confounds human language.

The image on the Tower card reminds us of the tale of Rapunzel.

All these images describe destruction, an idea that conveys the card's usual meanings. But we can also look at this card in a different way, as the lightning flash of revelation – the lightning releases us from the illusion we carry with us of normal consciousness.

These are all very grand themes. In normal usage we can think of the lightning as a more conventional kind of revelation, as some kind of discovery that unlocks a secret or ends an illusion under which we are laboring.

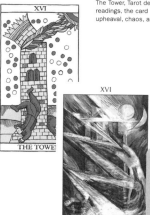

The Tower, Tarot de Marseilles. In readings, the card means upheaval, chaos, and conflict.

Tower, Tarot of the Spirit. The lightning traces the path of the sephiroth on the Kabbalist Tree of Life.

THE TOWER

The Tower, Haindl Tarot. The picture symbolizes the destructive blindness of modern civilization.

The Tower, Morgan-Greer Tarot. Energy bursts from within.

Persephone, Queen of the Underworld, who divides her time between the world of the living and the world of the dead.

In readings, this card usually means chaos, upheaval, conflict. Something shatters a long-standing situation. Usually, however, the situation has "imprisoned" the person, so that the chaos releases him. Alternatively, the card may indicate some revelation, either joyous or disturbing.

Reversed, we fight against the destruction of our "tower." We hang on to what we know, despite the sense of it falling down around us. The Tower reversed can indicate a milder version of chaos. But it also may show the situation going on longer.

the star

After the storm, the calm. When we clear things out in our lives, we feel at ease. Free and whole in a way we may never have known. The Fool has faced the Devil, has called down the lightning flash and now enters the realm of the Stars, a place of hope and healing.

We find resemblances to Temperance here – two vessels of water, one foot on land, one on water. Instead of pouring liquid back and forth between cups, the Star maiden pours it out freely, as if she gives life to the world. And instead of an angel, a vision of the divine within the self, we see a naked woman, open to her own humanity.

Just as the Empress two rows above suggested the "grain mother" Demeter, so the Star evokes her daughter

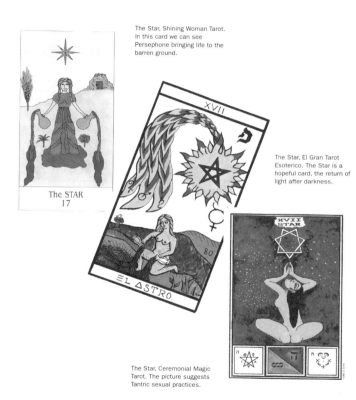

The Star, Shining Woman Tarot. In this card we can see Persephone bringing life to the barren ground.

The Star, El Gran Tarot Esoterico. The Star is a hopeful card, the return of light after darkness.

The Star, Ceremonial Magic Tarot. The picture suggests Tantric sexual practices.

Persephone, who every year goes down to the dark underworld of the dead and then returns. At the end of the Mysteries, the celebrants poured water from two large vessels into cracks in the Earth. In the Shining Woman Tarot we see Persephone bringing life to the thirsty ground.

In the fairy tale, Rapunzel heals the prince's blindness with her own tears. In that same spirit the Star maiden pours out her waters of love – on land, that is as action in the world, and back into the water, to ripple the unconscious. Between the Empress and the Star comes the Wheel of Fortune. There we saw a symbolic version of the cycles of time. Here we experience renewal directly in our own lives.

The Star is Seventeen (1+7=8), Strength. That gentle passion gets its fullest expression in the Star.

In readings, this card speaks to us of hope, optimism, and bright prospects. She brings calm and confidence in the future. In a crisis or afterward, the Star promises release and new life.

Reversed, we allow doubt and insecurity to close off that natural belief in life. Something needs clearing up so that the person can free herself.

Remember that a reversed card contains the promise of the card's fulfillment. We only need to release the block to turn the Star the right way around.

JOURNEY TO THE LIGHT

the moon

After the upheaval of the Tower we find ourselves in a place
of peace. But our Fool cannot rest there, for she or he must
find a way to bring this inner opening back to the world of
daily life. Between the quiet night of the Star and the bright
day of the Sun lies the half-light of the Moon. Once more
we find a path between two pillars. It begins at the pool of
the unconscious and moves through hidden ways. The
Moon leads us on an unknown journey, one of instincts,
dreams, myths, and primal emotions.

The card comes at the center of the line, the test card, like
the Emperor and Justice above it. These cards treated
more human subjects, issues of society and an
assessment of our lives. The Moon goes deeper. We see
no people in the card, only animals, for the Moon's
reflected light stirs something very deep in our evolutionary
history. We have all heard how police and hospital
emergency rooms brace themselves during the full Moon
period. The stories of werewolves may originate with the
effect of the full Moon on normally "civilized" people.

Despite all its disturbances, the Moon also brings calm if
we accept the cyclic rhythms it creates in our bodies. Lunar
power only really frightens us if we try to convince
ourselves that we are only rational "solar" creatures with
no emotions or instinctive drives.

People have long believed that a
full Moon stirs the human
psyche.

The Moon, Charles VI Tarot. It symbolizes psychic awakening.

The Moon, Alchemical Tarot. The dog was the companion of the moon goddess Diana.

The Moon, Motherpeace Tarot emphasizes the menstrual cycle.

Because the menstrual period follows the Moon, women may experience the Moon's psychic power more directly than men. But men too need to accept that they are creatures of instinct connected to nature.

In readings the Moon may indicate a psychic awakening. Intuition, dreams, and imagination all become stronger. If we accept these things we enrich our lives. The Moon can show a difficult emotional journey, especially when it appears with cards that show outer struggle, such as the breakup of a relationship.

When the card is reversed, the Moon shows us resisting its power. We ignore our dreams, or try to suppress intuition or psychic flashes. This may lead to anxiety, anger, or emotional outbursts.

To use its power positively, we need to turn the Moon symbolically right side up through acceptance of all sides of ourselves.

the sun

After the fearsome journey of the Moon we come to the joyous Sun. In the sunlight, everything becomes clear and direct. The Kabbalist letter for the Moon, *Kaph,* meant the back of the head, the most ancient part of our brain. The letter for the Sun, *Resh,* means the entire head, but especially the front, with its neo-cortex, or gray matter, that makes us human. The cortex is the area of rational consciousness.

The brightly shining Sun brings clarity into our lives.

Waite altered the traditional form of the card to show a naked babe riding forth from a garden. The usual image depicts two children, often with a wall behind them, as if they stand inside a sanctuary. Male and female in most decks, they hold hands. The opposites of life have joined together. Once again, the cards seem to mirror the story of Rapunzel, for when Rapunzel heals her prince with her tears and he can see again (the light returns, as in the card of the Sun) he discovers they have children, a boy and a girl. (Note that the Tarot does not come from the fairy tale, or vice versa. Both originate in the universal story of the development of human consciousness.)

The Sun comes below the Hierophant and the Hanged Man. The Hierophant instructs his disciples how to live their lives. The Hanged Man reverses outer values and finds a personal connection to life. In the Sun, that connection shines brightly in our daily lives and relationships. The image of the children with the Sun above them returns us once more to that triangular structure we first saw in the Hierophant. Now we see a genuine union of the two lower figures.

When the Sun appears in a reading, we can expect happiness, contentment and success. Problems get resolved, people come together, everything looks simpler and clearer. The person can think better and see solutions. The Sun shows a time of energy and optimism. If it appears with the Magician, the person can channel that energy into creative projects.

The Sun, Visconti Sforza Tarot. The Sun shows a time of energy and success.

The Sun, Thoth Tarot. Radiant energy fills the card.

XIX — THE SUN

Reversed, the Sun does not set but becomes clouded over. In other words, the happiness and positive energy remain, but some of the clarity gets lost. It may be necessary for the person to acknowledge consciously life's blessings.

The Sun, Morgan Greer Tarot. Two children stand before a wall symbolizing security.

THE GREAT AWAKENING

We have seen many variations on the three-part structure, from the Hierophant to the Sun. In Judgement we see something new, a child between the man and woman. The opposites have created and brought something into the world. The child stands with its back to us, for we do not know yet what form this new consciousness will take.

The name of this card derives from the Christian Last Judgment, when Gabriel's horn summons the dead from their graves. There is a significant difference here. No one is being judged. We see no miserable souls condemned to Hell. Instead, all the figures rise up together. Paul Foster Case criticized Waite for including extra people in the background. However, Judgement is essentially a social image, for when any single person achieves such an awakening it affects everyone around him or her. Judgement comes below the card of Death. In Death we saw the end of something. In Judgement we see renewal in the image of resurrection.

The number Twenty reduces to Two, the High Priestess. There we saw the water of the unconscious behind her curtain. Here the souls rise out of water into a consciousness that does not isolate itself from inner truth. Along with the Two, the other number in Twenty is Zero. Our Fool has learned maturity and wisdom. Now he returns to his childlike wonder as he opens wide his arms to life.

The Last Judgment; Gabriel calls the dead from their graves. Unlike the Tarot card, many are condemned to Hell.

Above right
Judgement, Charles VI Tarot. In this card, the trumpet calls a whole group of people to a new beginning.

Right
Judgement, Elemental Tarot. This card calls us to forgive and repent.

The most important symbol in this card is not any of the people or the angel, but the trumpet. Something calls to us. It tells us that the time has come to rise to a new existence. When we follow this "call" everything changes.

When people see this card in a reading they often look at the title and think it requires them to judge something. They may think of the card as a condemnation. The picture suggests something very different. The image of resurrection tells you to acknowledge a wonderful change. It does not say you should change, or even that you can change, but that you already have changed in some deep way. The trumpet has sounded in your very soul and a new life opens before you.

Reversed, we resist this idea. We make excuses why we cannot follow our genuine knowledge that our lives have shifted. The basic meaning, however, remains the same.

Now the Fool achieves the final "victory," the culmination of his journey. For many, the end of the Major Arcana means a new beginning, like a spiral that returns but to a higher level. This is true if we see the World card as just another state of being. But we can see this particular card as an opening to a whole new existence, as if we have traveled along a path in a cave all our lives, and suddenly emerge into the wide world. We call it the World, and in some decks the Universe, because we understand fully our connection to all existence. With every breath we take we receive oxygen from the plants and give them carbon dioxide in return. All the molecules in our body, as well as everything else on our planet, originally came from the dust of exploding stars millions of years ago. The person who truly experiences the World card knows these things in the very way she or he moves.

The dancer holds two wands, lightly. Where the Magician needed to put his full attention into the proper use of his power, and the High Priestess sat very still to keep her sense of mystery, the World dances easily.

The Tarot de Marseilles and subsequent decks show the dancer as a woman. In fact, just as the Fool is really an androgyne, so the World dancer is in fact a hermaphrodite (as can be seen in El Gran Tarot Esoterico). The difference between the two is that an androgyne can potentially express both male and female. The hermaphrodite,

The World, Tarot de Marseilles. This card signifies success and fulfillment.

however, fulfills that potential, not magically in a bodily transformation, but in everything that she or he does.

Twenty-one turns around Twelve. The World liberates the Hanged Man, who no longer needs to cling tightly to the branch, for he knows now that the Tree of Life is growing within him. It springs forth at every step of the dance.

The World is a wonderful card to receive in any reading, for it signifies success, abundance, fulfillment. In a difficult situation, the person dances lightly, sure of everything she or he does.

Reversed does not mean failure, but rather stagnation. A great promise remains for the querent but she or he needs to take some action to release it.

The World, El Gran Tarot Esoterico. The dancer in this card is a hermaphrodite.

At the end of his journey the Fool becomes at one with the World. Here, a nebula mirrors the image on the World card.

Despite differences in interpretation, the Major Arcana have followed a distinct line of development, and we are able to discern the clear connections between the oldest decks and the most recent ones. The Minor Arcana, however, presents a very different situation. Until the Golden Dawn, virtually no Tarot deck had attempted to give the pip cards symbolic imagery, so that card readers who used them had to interpret them according to arbitrary formulas.

the minor arcana

Pip Cards

The Golden Dawn itself did not show actual scenes on the pip cards; the pictures displayed geometric arrangements of the suit emblems with hints toward meaning in such things as the way water flows from one Cup to another, or the way the hands grip the Swords. More important, they developed a fundamental concept for each card based on the element and the number.

Later card designers, especially Waite and Smith, used themes such as these to create more explicit pictures, and the majority of modern decks now use Smith's Rider pictures as the basis for their imagery. As we go through the pip cards we will use several decks to represent different approaches.

the visconti-sforza

The oldest known deck is also one of the most elegant. Its ornate pip cards show us the formal tradition. Despite their lack of symbolism, they still attract cartomancers who prefer set formulas as meanings for each card.

the rider-waite

Without this deck, the Tarot's worldwide popularity probably never would have happened. Besides all the copies the deck itself has sold, and all the "clones" it has generated

The pip cards of the Visconti-Sforza deck are elegant and formal.

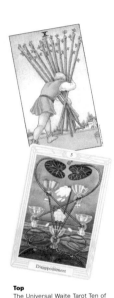

(a Rider clone is a deck that copies its imagery very
closely), it has inspired countless artists to take the Minor
cards in new directions. The Universal Waite deck has been
used here as it is both contemporary and is still very close
to the original design. Some Tarotists dislike the Rider-
Waite's influence, pointing out that many card interpreters
and designers think Waite and Smith invented the pictures
out of nothing, or even that the Tarot did not exist before
them. The Rider-Waite deck is less than a hundred years
old, they argue, so why make it the main line of tradition?
Why not go back to its sources in Kabbalah? In answer, we
can point out that the Kabbalah tradition in Tarot goes back
only a few decades before the Rider-Waite. More important,
while people certainly should learn the source of the ideas
behind the Rider cards, Smith's pictures are a genuine
creation inspiring a modern tradition.

the thoth

Lady Frieda Harris' pictures for Aleister Crowley give us a
different realization of the Golden Dawn system. Like
Mathers' original designs, they stay close to geometry but
they elaborate the thematic ideas in an elegant style that
brings a modernist contrast to the Visconti-Sforza. The
Thoth cards also originated a widespread modern practice,
the use of theme words written directly on the card. The
titles follow the Golden Dawn titles (with a few changes).
They help readers to find the meaning in the abstract
pictures. Some readers find them distracting and cut them
off. At the other extreme, people who find Crowley's

explanations too dense or just dislike his ideas have reinterpreted the pictures entirely, using the theme words on the cards as a starting point.

the alchemical tarot

This recent deck shows the way modern Tarot designers play off the Rider-Waite images. While they follow an ancient system (one that may have helped to inspire the original Tarot pictures), Robert Place's Alchemical cards often show an awareness of Pamela Smith without ever copying her. In the Four of Coins, for example, where the Rider picture showed a king holding on tightly to his golden disks, the Alchemical version shows a man burying his treasure.

the elemental tarot

This modern deck shows the possibility of a self-contained system that is independent of the Rider cards. Though Caroline Smith and John Astrop show Golden Dawn influence, they returned to the basic meanings of the elements and the numbers to create a structure for Smith's stylized and witty drawings. The deck also illustrates a modern practice of assigning a god or goddess to every card.

Unlike some decks that do this, the pictures in the Elemental Tarot do not actually show the particular mythological character. Their names, however, provide an extra kind of reference, and a way for the Tarot to reach out to a wider world.

Top
The Elemental Tarot returns to the basic meanings of the elements.

Above
Four of Coins, Alchemical Tarot brings fresh imagery to the ideas in the cards.

ACES – KETHER (CROWN)

The Aces form the root of each suit, the element in its pure form. The Kabbalists described the Tree of Life as growing downward, with its roots in heaven above and its branches reaching into our world of daily life. Aces become both the root and the crown of each Tree.

In the Waite deck all four Aces come to us held out by a hand immersed in a cloud. The four Aces act like a gift, as if life says to us, "Here, experience the eagerness of Wands, the emotion of Cups, the sharp intelligence of Swords, the wealth of Pentacles."

The Kabbalists believed that in each of the four worlds there are 10 emanations, or sephiroth. The ace is the highest sephirah, the Kether or "Crown", in each of the four suits.

In the first three we see drops fall – buds in Wands, water in Cups, light in Swords. They all form *yods,* the first letter of God's name, and a symbol of divine grace. These gifts come to us not as a reward for virtue, but simply as experience. The exception is Pentacles, suit of physical reality.

Because these come to us as gifts of life, we cannot expect such gifts to last forever. If the Aces show up in our Tarot reading, we should make certain that we pay special attention to the opportunities that these cards reveal. It is very important that we are careful not to take such opportunities too much for granted.

The Suits

ace of wands

The Ace of Wands gives us the energy of life itself. Without Fire, the spark of creation, we would become like empty machines. The *yods* fall like leaves bursting from the branch. This Ace gives us power, excitement, sexual desire, eagerness to go out and see the world. It signals the enthusiasm to begin new projects. Someone under the influence of this card may overwhelm others.

Reversed, the surge of Wands Fire becomes hard to control. The person may experience chaos, or the collapse of projects. The person may become listless, or scatter his strength on false starts without the patience to follow them through.

ACE of WANDS.

The Aces are all giving cards. In the Universal Waite Tarot, they appear presented to us in a hand surrounded by a cloud.

ace of cups

Fire gives life to the world, but Water – love – gives it meaning. The Ace of Cups brings happiness. The image suggests the primal feminine in the way the Wand symbolizes the masculine. The feminine part of sexuality allows us (men as well as women) to receive the forceful desire of Fire. The Waite picture *(below)* shows the Holy Grail. The image of the dove and wafer goes back to the very earliest Tarot decks. In the stories of King Arthur, it was not the army that held together the realm, but the presence of the Grail. Love, not power, rules our lives.

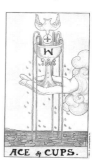

ACE of CUPS.

Reversed, the emotions become distorted. Jealousy interrupts love, or we ignore happiness.

ace of swords

This is the Ace of the mind, in many ways the most powerful. Our culture tends to value energy, emotion, and wealth, but without intellect we could not make sense of any of them. The Ace of Swords conveys power in virtually every deck. In the Waite *(see below)* we see mountains in the background, symbol of abstract thought. The Sword points straight up for commitment to truth. It pierces a crown, the way the mind sees through events and actions to understand the principles within them.

The gift of this Ace allows us to think clearly. It also helps us to plan ahead and work for the future and carry out projects. It may indicate sternness and high principles.

Reversed brings illusions, difficulty in thinking, anger, exaggeration. The person needs to think more carefully.

The gift of reality. The magic of nature. Security. Wealth. All these things come to us through this Ace. With any question about business or creative projects, the Ace of Pentacles promises success. The Waite *(see right)* image hints that these things are a starting point in our quest for a worthwhile life. We see this in the gate that opens to the mountains. The oval shape of the gate reminds us of the wreath around the World dancer, another card of success.

Reversed, the Ace of Pentacles does not indicate loss, but rather difficulties around money or other material issues. The person may worry about the future, or get caught up in her own greed or other people's jealousy. Alternatively, the person may need to leave a safe environment and venture out boldly into the world.

ACE of PENTACLES

The oval shape of the gate in the Ace of Pentacles is reminiscent of the wreath in the World dancer.

XXI

THE WORLD.

TWOS – CHOKMAH (WISDOM)

The movement from One to Two takes a giant step of awareness. One is absolute, unqualified. Two creates a partner and a reflection. Two takes us from principles to actual experience – we see people doing something in the Waite and other decks. The Twos create duality and the possibility of opposition.

They also open the way for dialogue and relationships. The Kabbalists speak of the original Adam – and even God – as hermaphroditic. Both needed to separate male and female in order to create the possibilities of communication and balance.

The Bible tells us that God created Eve so that Adam would have a partner.

Different decks handle the theme of communication differently. In the Elemental Tarot we see stages of relationships. In Fire (Wands) we see two figures drawn to each other, as if by the fire of their personalities. With Water (Cups) we see a couple about to embrace. Air (Swords) pushes the people apart. They wear masks and look at each other suspiciously. The Earth suit (Pentacles) shows one figure only, but he seems to balance different ways to express himself. The Alchemical Tarot shows the impact of Two. In Wands, the fiery torch from the cloud ignites a tree. The Cups shows a couple and a rose in an alchemical device. The Swords show conflict as the two Swords cross, but the owl, symbol of wisdom, indicates they can learn from each other. The Pentacle card is more arcane, with a lion swallowing the head of an eagle.

The Suits

Wands have a single-minded drive. This makes the Two and its complexity uncomfortable. The Waite picture *(see below left)* shows a successful man who holds the World in his hand. But it's a very small World – he looks out beyond the walls of his success to the excitement of unknown challenges. Waite spoke of the sadness of Alexander, who wept when he had conquered the known world, because he could not think of what else to do. The person with this card may need to learn to share his success with others.

Reversed, he decides to seek new adventure. He may give up past success in order to try new things.

The Two of Wands, from the Alchemical Tarot. Fiery energy passes from one source to another.

The angel from the Lovers card in the Universal Waite Tarot subtly reappears in the winged lion of the Two of Cups.

The emotional suit goes well with communication, duality, and reflection. The Waite shows a young couple pledging their love to each other *(see left)*. In contrast to the Lovers, this card indicates the beginning of a relationship. The separate souls entwine their energies, like the snakes of the caduceus. The winged lion head recalls the angel on the Lovers. Genuine emotion gives wings to sexual passion.

Reversed, something goes wrong with the ideal love envisioned in the card. Anger may come between the people, or distrust. Or, perhaps, what seemed like true love has revealed itself as but a mere infatuation.

With Swords, communication raises the idea of conflict. A further theme of Two is balance, and here the person seeks balance by avoiding communication. In the Elemental, people move away from each other. The Waite woman *(see left)* has tied a blindfold over her eyes so she will not have to look at anyone. She holds the Swords at her shoulders as if to strike anyone who tries to approach her. Notice the way the Swords block the heart and lungs. A more positive view of this image suggests that she closes off outside stimulation to communicate with her own psychic truth.

Reversed, she either loses her balance – stress tips her over into the choppy water – or else she opens herself to others.

Here, too, balance becomes the issue. The person seems to juggle different needs or desires. Work or study may conflict with pleasure. He does not set them carefully in a scale and weigh them, but instead tries to keep them in motion. And he dances, for this is fundamentally a card in which a person greatly enjoys his life.

Reversed, the conflicts become stronger, the demands and pressures harder to keep up in the air. The person may pretend to enjoy himself but secretly would like to drop everything. This meaning becomes stronger if the reading contains such cards as the Hermit – or the Two of Swords.

Far left
The Waite image of the Twos shows how the themes of communication and balance translate through the suit.

Left
The Two of Pentacles is renamed "The Plant" in the Elemental Tarot. The picture borrows imagery from the Rider version.

THREES – BINAH (UNDERSTANDING)

Three of Pentacles, Golden Dawn Tarot. The wheels contain crosses.

One + two = three. The fundamental numbers produce a child, that is, a basic fulfillment of the energy. One and Two exist in a kind of tension. Three resolves that tension by producing something. Look at the names and pictures on the Thoth cards, derived from the Golden Dawn. Wands optimism acts in the world as Virtue. The Cups overflow with Abundance. The Swords, with their theme of Sorrow, might seem the opposite of fulfillment. But if we think of Swords as instruments of conflict and (emotional) pain, what would fulfill them more than Sorrow?

The Suits

three of wands

Wands seek activity and challenges. They involve themselves in the world, especially in a career. They do not do this so much for money or prestige as for the excitement. Nevertheless, they achieve things and find themselves in positions of power. In the Waite picture *(see top right)* a man stands firmly on a hilltop and watches boats sail beneath him. Either he orders them out on a fresh expedition or they return with the rewards of past achievements. The card indicates someone in a strong position. He stands firmly, controlling the territory around him. He may seek new challenges, but this is from a secure position.

Reversed, the person loses some of that sense of accomplishment and security. He hesitates to try anything new, as the ground no longer feels solid beneath him. At the same time, his doubts may open him up to working with others. The reversed Three of Wands sometimes means cooperation in business.

three of cups

This is one of the most joyous cards in the Tarot. The Alchemical gives the picture a more stately quality but still suggests fullness as each woman bears an urn with one of the elements on her head, with the card itself as Water. The Rider presents celebration and friendship *(see below right)*.

A feminine quality comes through in all these pictures. Emotional sharing, open expression of feelings, cooperation without someone in charge, are characteristics we often associate with women.

The Three of Cups speaks of celebration, friendship, family, and help given freely and with love. Life is good and people share their happiness. In contrast to the Two of Cups, the Three of Cups involves friendship more than romance.

Reversed may indicate a loss of happiness or a disappointment. Friendships become strained by hard times, or by envy and mistrust.

The Three of Cups is the card of friendship.

three of swords

In most decks, this is one of the most difficult cards. The
Lord of Sorrow, as the Golden Dawn called it. The
Elemental gives us an interesting alternative. In the Three
of Air we see a calm face in contemplation of a rolled-up
scroll. The fish-shaped eyes and winged brows suggest
knowledge of soul and spirit. The image on his forehead
comes from an Egyptian symbol for knowledge. Not just
sorrow but intellect fulfills the element of Air.

In the Waite *(see left)* deck we also see a hint of
intellect, for despite its pain, the picture appears
balanced, even calm. If we can accept the sorrow that
pierces our heart we can hope to understand and fully
accept it.

Reversed, we resist the pain of taking our sorrow into our
heart. We try to distract ourselves, and may become
confused, or emotionally cold. Such avoidance may prevent
healing.

three of pentacles

We think of Pentacles, originally Coins, as symbols of
wealth, so that we would expect the Threes to show
prosperity. The suit, however, involves us in the material
world in all its aspects, not just the accumulation of money
and property. The Kabbalist theme for this number is
Knowledge, and we know this element more deeply through
work than success.

The Alchemical shows an artist, peaceful in his concentration *(see below center)*. The Waite also shows an artist *(see below left)*, this time at work in a church, but here we see him with others, a monk to signify spiritual value, and the church architect to represent technical knowledge. When these things combine we get true mastery and accomplishment.

Reversed, the card slides toward mediocrity. A person does not do his best, either out of laziness, or a lack of commitment to the task. There may also be a lack of cooperation.

The Three of Air, Elemental Tarot. A serene figure contemplates a rolled-up scroll.

Detail from Four of Wands, Thoth Tarot. This card symbolizes harmony in a family or work situation.

FOURS – CHESED (LOVE)

One, two, and three have a fundamental quality. When we move beyond them we come to more complex ideas. With Four, we get the idea of structure and order. The image of a square somehow suggests stability (and dullness). We find this in our language, with expressions like "a square meal" and "fair and square."

The forms on the Thoth Four of Disks evoke solidity as well as the card's theme of Power. Where the Threes expanded into such themes as Abundance and Sorrow, the Fours now define and set boundaries.

The theme of order and structure does not have to mean repression. We need structure to help us to define our lives. Four refers to our arms and legs, and the four directions of the compass, all of which establish our physical sense and experience of the world around us.

The Suits

four of wands

We saw with the Two of Swords how a suit may work against a number. Wands – Fire – love freedom and openness. Any structure to Wands may seem like a gray stone wall. The Waite *(see left)* shows a pair of celebrants leading a parade out of a city. They do not proceed toward an empty space, but toward the simplest of structures, garlands of flowers strung from four poles. We might think of it as a wedding canopy (marriage structures love). The Alchemical shows a man and woman embracing, with four torches behind them.

This card speaks to us of harmony between people in a family, a relationship, or work environment – that is, a structured situation. Enthusiasm fills the people so that others follow them. There may be something specific to celebrate.

Waite describes the Four of Wands card as unchanged when reversed, as if nothing could dampen its good spirits.

four of cups

Water does not like containment any more than Fire. The natural state of Water is flow. The Elemental version *(see below right)* shows the serene face that a person presents to the world. In the square, however, a panicky face reveals a secret claustrophobia. By contrast, the Thoth image shows four Cups filled to the brim with luxury, as if they can hardly hold the card's pleasure.

The Waite picture *(see above right)* shows a different response to structured emotion. A man sits with three Cups before him. He looks bored, as if life has become dull. A hand emerges with a new Cup, symbol of fresh experience. However, apathy now prevents him from looking up.

Reversed, the person shakes off his boredom. He discovers new opportunities that he hadn't noticed before. More importantly, he moves himself to take action.

Structure can refer to thoughts as well as buildings. In the Elemental Four of Air a square boxes in a part of a bird. A mind that labels and boxes everything may not even see the aspects of life that do not fit its preconceived ideas.

The Waite version *(see left)* emphasizes sorrow over intellect. It shows someone who retreats from pain or struggle in order to rest and heal. We might think of this card as isolation, flattened emotions, or hiding from the world. A church, however, is a place of healing. The stained-glass window shows Christ blessing a penitent. Withdrawal at the right time can allow a person to come back to life.

Reversed, the person ventures once more into the world. Isolation ends. Alternatively, a narrow-minded person begins to look beyond artificial boundaries of prejudice.

No element suits the theme of structure like the Earth, so solid and real. While the Thoth deck shows the power of physical reality, the Waite, Alchemical, and Elemental all emphasize security, in particular the security of possessions. The Waite *(see below)* and Elemental figures on the cards hold on tightly to their disks. The Alchemical goes so far as to bury his coins in the ground.

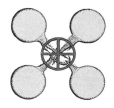

Detail from El Gran Esoterico Four of Pentacles.

People tend to view the Four of Pentacles negatively. They speak of his greed, the way he clings tightly to his possessions. The Waite king uses the Pentacles to shield himself from life. One sits on his crown to keep in his thoughts. He places two under his feet as if to keep out the environment. He holds the fourth over his body. And yet, in chaotic or dangerous situations, we may need just this kind of psychic barrier to give protection to ourselves from outside threats.

Reversed, he lets down his guard. A frightened person opens up to others. A greedy person learns to share his wealth.

The flaming fingers of the Five of Wands, Alchemical Tarot.

FIVES – GEBURAH (JUDGEMENT)

The fifth *sephirah* is a harsh one, involving life's painful realities. In most Tarot decks the Fives show aspects of sorrow and loss. Look at the theme words on the Thoth cards – Strife, Disappointment, Defeat, and Worry – or those on the Elemental – Furnace, Sudden Rain, Storm, Quake.

The Fours provided security and structure. We order our lives into a neat box. With Five, some outside influence breaks up this illusion of perfection. As with the Tower, this experience may feel like disaster, but it also can liberate us.

In bodily terms, Four appeared in our limbs. Five adds the head. It is consciousness that makes us human, but it also brings awareness of loss, fear, and emotional hurt.

The Suits

five of wands

Wands' optimism makes this the most positive of the Fives, especially in the Waite *(see left),* though the Alchemical, with its flaming fingers, gives more of a sense of power than "Strife." Even the Thoth picture shows the Wands in balance, while the Elemental's acrobatic woman gives the card a circus feel. Smith's picture shows a group of boys banging sticks together. This is a mock battle, for no one hits anyone else. This kind of conflict energizes rather than hurts. The card can mean healthy competition at work, or a vigorous debate, or relationship arguments that never become vicious.

Reversed, the situation becomes more unpleasant. People no longer fight by the rules, and the person may feel that someone has stabbed him or her in the back.

Disappointment

five of cups

The Thoth card *(see right)* demonstrates "Disappointment," with withered flowers and an upside-down Pentacle. The Alchemical shows three fallen pots. A gold liquid spills from one, like an alchemist's failed experiment. However, two birds fly upward, as if liberated. The Elemental, with its upside down woman, depicts "an awkward emotional situation."

The Waite *(see right),* like the Alchemical, seems to emphasize loss, but with hints of renewal. A shrouded woman looks sadly at three spilled Cups. She seems to have lost some great hope or joy. And yet, two Cups stand behind her. They represent the things in her life that remain, possibly love and support from friends and family.

Reversed, the person begins to recover from sorrow. In terms of the Waite scene, She discovers the two Cups and carries them over the bridge to her home for a fresh start.

This is one of the more disturbing cards in the deck, especially in the Waite *(see left)*. Notice also what looks like shattered glass in the Thoth deck *(see below)*. Only the Alchemical seems to take a positive view, showing a blacksmith making Swords, as if to prepare for a fight.

The Golden Dawn called this card "Lord of Defeat." The idea comes from the Fives' theme of loss joined to Swords conflict. The card addresses those moments in life when we feel broken and humiliated. The Elemental, however, hints that defeat can free us and allow us to "see things from a different angle."

Reversed, the fresh viewpoint begins to emerge. The person moves away from shame and despair. The reversed Five can suggest that the person might avoid a defeat through a change of plans.

Another disturbing card, though the Thoth title, "Worry" *(see below right)* implies that the problems may lie in our fear of the future as much as actual circumstances. Still, if we add the element of Earth to the number we find at least the fear of poverty and illness. But is that all there is? The Alchemist's one-legged beggar seems to stare at his empty hand and not see the coins lying on the ground. The woman in the Elemental card bends over despondently and does not notice the world at her feet.

And in the Waite *(see right)*, the miserable couple passes a church, a place of sanctuary, but they do not notice it. The card may depict a powerful bond between two people who suffer together.

Reversed, new prospects relieve the people's suffering. Life begins to improve. This may endanger a relationship based on mutual struggle against "the cruel world."

Worry

SIXES – TIPHERETH (BEAUTY)

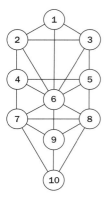

Six lies at the center of the Kabbalist Tree of Life, suggesting harmony and communication.

We can look at this card as a recovery after the stress of the Fives. The world seems to turn right again and new confidence emerges. The Elemental Six of Earth shows abundance, fertility, health, all the things that seemed lost in the Fives.

The center of the Tree of Life inspires ideas of harmony and communication. We get a similar idea when we think of Six as two times three, that is, generations. And yet, we also get a sense of hierarchy in these cards, especially in the Waite, where one person seems superior to the others. This too appears among generations, for the young need to find their own way. In the Alchemical Tarot, a young alchemist seems to challenge the gods themselves in the Six of Staffs.

In the Elemental Tarot, the Sixes are representative of Earth, here symbolized by Mother Earth.

The Suits

The Thoth card *(see below right)* calls this Victory, and on the Waite *(see right)* we see a man with a laurel wreath on his head. He rides a horse while his followers walk alongside. The Elemental goddess name for this card is Nike, famous for the statue of her as "Winged Victory." The face on the card wears a wreath, while a courageous lion crouches beneath him. He also, however, wears a mask, as if his power depends on presenting a confident face to the world. The positive Six and the energetic Wands produce not just Victory, but even more, the kind of self-confidence that inspires others.

Reversed, the mask slips and the person begins to doubt his powers. As a result, he may lose some of his followers.

One of the most delightful cards in most decks, the Six of Cups shows a happy union of the sephirah and the flowing Water of the suit. The Thoth deck *(see below left)* calls it Pleasure. Erzulie, the goddess of the Elemental, is the Haitian goddess of love and sensuality.

The Waite *(see left)* picture stresses nurturing as an older child helps a younger. Many see this card as looking back on happy childhood memories. At the same time, some have seen a disturbing quality. The child appears overprotected, too covered-up, as if unable to act on her own.

Reversed, the "Oasis" of "Pleasure" (combining the Elemental and Thoth titles) ends and we return to more difficult aspects of life. Alternatively, a person looks to the future instead of the past.

The Thoth deck calls this card "Lord of Science." Some people see this term negatively, as narrow materialism that denies spiritual reality. The picture seems to suggest constricting webs. But it also may show the way science illuminates the intricate connections of all life. The Elemental *(see right)* portrays the freedom of thought and the delight of discovery, both of which are themes that go well with Six.

Pamela Smith's picture *(see below right)* is one of her most mysterious. Ostensibly the card shows a journey. However, the people appear bowed down, silent, almost like dead souls ferried to a new life. They may carry some kind of family secret.

Reversed in the Waite version, people speak out. They no longer carry their Sword burdens in silence but confront issues. Other versions of the Tarot emphasize discoveries and new ideas.

Here too the Waite *(see left)* is slightly at odds with other decks. Thoth *(see below left)* features "Success," and the Elemental shows a bountiful "Harvest," symbolizing prosperity, but also general well-being and good company. In the Waite (and Elemental) we see themes of sharing. The Waite beggars have found a patron who measures out coins to them from a balanced scale (a symbol that evokes Justice). This is a good card to get if you ask about finding work, for it shows help from someone in power. Notice the return to the three-part structure we saw so often in the Major cards. Instead of a Hierophant we find a merchant. The card implies generosity but also inequality.

Reversed, the person may be blocking possible aid from someone. He may need the humility to ask others for help.

The confidence of the Six of Wands card may come from hiding behind a mask.

SEVENS — NETZACH (VICTORY)

The Sixes established stability after the difficult Fives. Now we need to open up our lives once more. The Sevens give us risk-taking, experimentation, and courage. The Kabbalistic idea of Victory (anticipated in the Six of Wands) and the masculine number stress the heroic approach to life. This does not always produce long-term results. The Victory may be temporary, or even more in the realm of fantasy.

Though each of the decks we are using (the Visconti-Sforza Tarot excepted) owes something to the Golden Dawn approach, they all vary the meanings. The Elemental Sevens involve some kind of risk. The Waite and the Alchemical both give a more positive meaning to the Earth suit. Where the Golden Dawn called it "Success Unfulfilled," the Waite shows a growing bush, and the Alchemical a symbol of that very fulfillment. The Thoth extends the theme to "Failure," and changes the Golden Dawn Cups theme of "Illusionary Success" to "Debauch," emphasizing sensuality.

Seven of Cups, Alchemical Tarot. This card emphasizes the process of creativity.

The Suits

The Golden Dawn called this card "Lord of Valour," and we see various images of courage and Wands' combativeness. We might even say that the number and the suit fit together too well, for the card becomes overbalanced toward aggressive approaches to problems. The Alchemical shows dogs at each others' throats, while the Thoth *(see top left)* displays a gnarled stick that seems to overpower the more elegant staffs behind it. And in the Waite *(see bottom left)* a strong man beats down all opposition. Only the Elemental *(see center left)* takes a gentler approach, with an unorthodox diver to symbolize a person who acts outrageously for the sake of change. Rather than trying to fight against the disapproval of other people he simply ignores them.

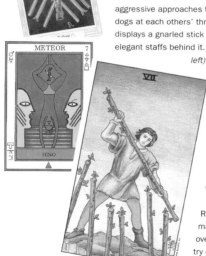

Reversed, the person's courage may fail, and life's problems may overwhelm him. However, he also may try out a less aggressive approach, especially in relationships.

The element of Water symbolizes love and imagination. Here the Thoth *(see below)* and Elemental emphasize the side of love (sensuality more in the Thoth), and the Waite *(see right)* and Alchemical the imagination. The Elemental shows someone attractive, who may play fast and loose with other people's imaginations as he moves from partner to partner. The dripping Cups in the Thoth picture evoke excess and "Debauch."

For the Alchemical and the Waite the issue becomes translating imagination into action. The Alchemical shows a choice between possibilities. The Waite picture shows a parade of fantasies. But if the person cannot ground them in action, they remain daydreams.

Reversed moves toward the necessary action. The person chooses from among various desires and begins to make the choice a reality.

Debauch

With the image of a Sword, we might expect a courageous hero. Swords, however, are the suit of mind rather than action. Called to the service of heroism and daring, Air formulates complex schemes to seek a Victory. The ultimate uselessness of such trickery comes out in the Thoth title of "Futility" *(see below)*. In the Waite *(see left)*, the idea of scheming appears in the smirk on the man's face, and also the fact that he has stolen five, not all seven, of the Swords. The Elemental shows us reckless action – he puts his head in a tiger's mouth – done for excitement and thrills.

Reversed, the person acts more carefully. He may stop and think, or get advice from others, before trusting some scheme or wild plan.

Futility

The Golden Dawn "Success Unfulfilled," which can mean postponement, goes further in the Thoth to become "Failure," a theme that seems in conflict with the positive tone of the number Seven. The Waite *(see below)* deck gives a more measured version, with a farmer who pauses in his work to look at what he has done. Some people see his gaze as satisfaction at the results of his hard work. He has reached a point where he can step back and trust that the bush (which may symbolize a career or a project or a relationship) will continue to grow and be healthy. Others, however, believe he frowns at all the work yet to do.

Reversed stresses the side of dissatisfaction. Work does not go well, or the goal is not clear. The person may need to look at what success or failure would mean to him or her.

EIGHTS – HOD (GLORY)

The Sevens broke up stability by taking risks. They sought the power of Netzach. Hod moves us to Glory, that is, recognition, especially in the Elemental, which stresses the idea of rewards for previous efforts. The other decks tend to stress movement toward goals. This may include consolidation, as in the Alchemical Eight of Staffs, where we see a worker cut back fiery trees. He knows what he needs to do and sets out to do it.

With Eight we see another example of the suit opposing the number. Swords conflict "interferes," to paraphrase the Thoth theme, with the idea of movement or accomplishment. In the Thoth deck we see the Swords like a fence closing in jagged energy. The Alchemical shows the "beast within" held by a line of disturbed thoughts. The Waite is the most vivid of the decks (as is so often the case), with its bound and blindfolded woman.

The figure in this Elemental Eight of Cups reaches to the "Well" of existence in meditation.

By contrast, unstable Fire calls forth a "Volcano."

The Suits

In the Thoth *(see right)* and Waite *(see below)* this card is
the image of movement itself. The Thoth calls it
"Swiftness" and sends lightning in every direction. The
Waite shows a more directed movement. The sticks, like
arrows, fly toward the ground, as if at a target. This
optimistic card indicates clear progress toward a goal.
If a person asks about a long-term project it will soon
achieve success, or a breakthrough. In romance
questions the Waite Eight of Wands can mean "arrows
of love." The Elemental takes

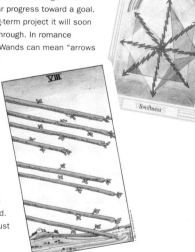

success a step further,
with an admired woman
perched on top of a
"Volcano." Her hard work
has brought recognition.
The Fire energy, however,
makes her position
unstable.

Reversed disrupts that clear
movement. Energy dissipates
as projects remain suspended.
Delays become possible, or just
lack of resolution. "Arrows of
jealousy " may replace love.

The Thoth calls this "Indolence" *(see center left)* as if Cups' lack of initiative makes movement difficult. Similarly, the Elemental shows someone deep in meditation. She has moved inward. The Alchemical shows a different kind of movement, as a potter loses himself in his craft.

The Waite image *(see top left)* reminds us that we can move away from goals as well as toward them. A man leaves eight Cups behind. Unlike the situation with the Fives, nothing has spilled. He simply knows the time has come to move on. Joined with the Hermit, or the High Priestess, he may be leaving a relationship.

Reversed, the Eight of Cups urges us to stay with a situation. It also may suggest that we remain involved in the world around us.

The Elemental considers this card respect for intellectual achievement. The other decks all show some kind of "interference." The Waite *(see bottom left)* shows a woman seemingly stopped in all ways. Ropes tie her so she cannot move, Swords surround her, a castle, symbol of authority, looms behind her, and a blindfold prevents her from seeing. But notice – no one from the castle is actually there to guard her, the Swords do not block her, and the ropes do not tie her legs. The only thing that truly stops her is the blindfold, that is, confusion. The person with this card has more possibilities than she realizes. Possibly she has let someone else convince her that she is helpless.

Reversed, movement becomes possible through clear thought and careful analysis of the situation. In terms of the Waite picture, she works off the blindfold and takes her first steps.

eight of pentacles

Movement slows down for the suit of Earth, but it also produces real achievements. "Prudence" in the Thoth *(see bottom right)* shows a carefully grown tree, heavy with fruit. The Elemental figure, with its firmly planted feet, and its orderly gold disks, four on each side, emphasizes the results of hard work. Both the Alchemical *(see right)* and the Waite *(see top right)* show the work itself rather than the reward. This is where the movement of Pentacles/Coins lies, in the development of skills. Compared to the artistic flair of the Alchemical Eight of Cups, the workers on both cards do not seek to create individual works of art. Instead, they perfect their craft by making the same coin over and over. This can be a card of learning a skill.

Reversed, the person becomes impatient. He allows fantasies of success to interfere with the hard work and skill needed to achieve true success.

NINES – YESOD (FOUNDATION)

The last single digit number gives us a sense of completion. If we think of the nine months of pregnancy we can say that the essential quality of the suit comes fully to life here. The Thoth names all describe some issue fundamental to that suit – "Strength" for Wands, "Happiness" for Cups, "Cruelty" for Swords, "Gain" for Pentacles. The terms simplify more complex Golden Dawn phrases – "Great Strength," "Material Happiness," "Despair and Cruelty," and "Material Gain." The Thoth cards have pared these down to their essence and joined them to pictures as formal as the Visconti-Sforza.

The Nines, the last single digit card, suggests a sense of completion, reminding us of the nine months of human pregnancy.

The Alchemical also emphasizes simplicity, especially in the beautiful tree on the Nine of Coins. The Elemental describes the number Nine as the moment when we find "the real values" of the suit. Here too the cards are strong and direct.

The Waite chooses complexity. We can clearly see the relation to the Golden Dawn themes. The cards show us the fulfillment of the suit. But they also show us a price we pay to achieve the different qualities.

The Suits

In the Thoth the single Wand, with its radiant Sun at the
top, dominates all the others. The Elemental title,
"Radiance," shows a serene face of someone secure in her
beliefs. Yet here too she overpowers the figure
beneath her. The mysterious Alchemical
implies that we find our Strength by giving
something up, for it shows a wolf that has
been sacrificed to the flame of
transformation.

The Waite *(see right),* too, shows
someone powerful and dominant. He
stands firmly with his stick, and looks
warily at the sticks lined up behind him.
But notice the tension in his shoulders,
the bandage around his head. A
forceful Wands approach to life
demands that he always remain
guarded, ready to fight at any
moment.

Reversed, the person's strength
may fail. Problems can overwhelm
him. However, the reversed card
also can offer the chance for a gentler
approach.

In the Thoth picture *(see below)* golden happiness pours from lotuses to overflow the Cups. The Elemental is both lush and simple, with the Greek Earth goddess Gaia bringing unconditional love and happiness, the deepest value of Water. The Waite *(see left)* shows a more superficial happiness, related to the excess implied in the Thoth card. We see a smug satisfied man before an array of Cups. He has chosen pleasure and contentment. This card can mean a good time, parties.

Reversed, the person may look beyond pleasure for deeper happiness. This holds especially for the Waite Tarot, for Waite gives "truth, loyalty, liberty" as the reversed meanings.

Happiness

In most decks this is one of the harshest cards. Even the Elemental, which emphasizes clear thought as the values of Air, calls it "Thunder" and shows a dead animal as the card's negative side. Other images, especially the Thoth *(see below)*, emphasize the painful aspect of a suit whose emblem is a weapon. We also find the Sword's mental side, for "Cruelty" is an attitude as well as an action. We see anxiety in the Alchemical, and anguish in the Waite.

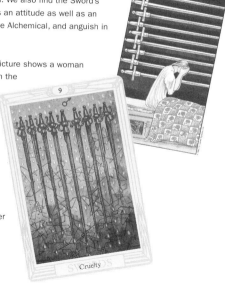

The vivid Waite *(see right)* picture shows a woman weeping in a dark night, with the Swords of her pain and sorrow above her. The card may symbolize some longstanding problem we can no longer ignore.

Reversed, the person tries to go beyond the pain or cruelty. She needs to make sure she truly changes the situation rather than deny her sadness.

Cruelty

A simpler and happier card. In the Elemental, people celebrate and dance. The Alchemical gives us a lush tree ready for harvest, the Thoth *(see below)* radiates in all directions. The Waite too *(see left)* appears very positive, for we see a woman in a fruitful garden. The garden is hers, and she has grown it through hard work. The hooded falcon symbolizes the discipline that has allowed her to create a good life for herself. This is a card of property and satisfaction. And yet, she is alone. She may have sacrificed relationships, or pleasure, in order to work in her "garden."

Reversed may mean a lack of discipline about work or career or money. It also can mean a new concern for relationships.

TENS – MALKUTH (KINGDOM)

The number Ten ends the cycle at the same time that it begins another. This double-sided condition may generate extreme states, as if situations need to go as far as possible before a new beginning. Compare the themes of the Tens in the Thoth Tarot with the Nines. "Pleasure" becomes "Satiety." "Cruelty" leads to "Ruin." "Gain" becomes "Wealth." Only in Wands does the title turn against the lower card, from "Strength" to "Oppression," as if the strength becomes inadequate.

The Alchemical shows the four suits at their most powerful. The power of Flames becomes the immortal Phoenix. The Vessels unify, as all emotions flow together. The Swords show a scene similar to the Waite, while the Coins give us the clever image of someone so obsessed with wealth that his money literally blinds him.

The Elemental stresses the passing of perfection. The cards all show collapse of their element. This breakdown of structures can lead to new possibilities.

Ten of Wands, Alchemical Tarot. The phoenix appears here in its most basic form.

In alchemy the power of the flames is transformed into the immortal bird, the phoenix.

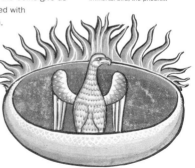

The Suits

To understand how "Strength" can become "Oppression," think of someone who uses his strength to endure an unpleasant situation – a bad marriage or an oppressive job.

Until the oppression becomes too much for the strength he will not make a change. The Waite image *(see left)* shows someone who accepts all the burdens of a situation, often without even a complaint. Inside, however, the person continues to suffer. The Elemental *(see below)* exposes the instability of such a situation and shows an outburst of long-suppressed anger.

Reversed, the person attempts to free himself from oppression, perhaps before it reaches an explosion of anger. In the Waite, he drops the sticks. Symbolically, it depends on whether he sets them down behind and walks away, free, or throws them down in a momentary fit, only to pick them up and continue his weary way once more.

The number theme of complete fulfillment works best with Cups, the suit of love. Thoth calls it "Satiety" *(see below)*. The Golden Dawn termed it "Perfected Success." Most decks follow the joyous theme shown in the Waite *(see right)* and the Alchemical. The latter presents its message symbolically, as an alchemical process, but the Waite gives us a very direct image. Happiness does not lie in fame or wealth, but in a loving family and a simple home.

Reversed, some outside influence may disturb the happiness. It also may indicate a person who does not recognize the happiness that he already has in his life.

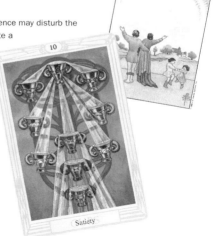

Satiety

In many decks the most fearsome card, the Ten of Swords carries the Swords theme of conflict and mental difficulties to an extreme. It takes only one Sword to kill a person. Here we see ten, whether in the back, like the Waite *(see left)* or the chest, like the Alchemical. The Elemental titles it "Cyclone" *(see below left)* and gives it the god name of a Guatemalan deity, Hurukan, from whom we get our word for hurricane, the most destructive of storms.

The very extremity gives us a clue to release from the turmoil. The overkill suggests an overreaction. The clear thought of the Ace has given way to panic. Notice in the Waite that the water remains calm and we can see light below the black clouds. Things are not as bad as they seem.

Reversed, the person gains a more balanced perspective. He takes steps to change the conditions but must be careful that relief is not merely temporary.

Ten of Swords, Alchemical Tarot. This fearsome card carries the theme of conflict and mental difficulties to an absurd extreme.

The suit of material goods finds its fulfillment in wealth and security. In the Thoth deck, the gold disks form a Tree of Life that lies amid a pile of money. The same Kabbalistic form overlays the Waite *(see right)* version. The everyday world of home and work contains a magic greater than all our spells and rituals.

And yet, the people in the Waite cards do not see the Pentacles Tree. Blindness or refusal to see also appear in the Elemental *(see right)* and Alchemical versions. Security can seem boring, and we may not recognize the value of what we have.

Reversed, the person seeks change and adventure and may take risks with financial or domestic security.

DESERT

10

TELEPINU

For the modern Tarot designer, the court cards have presented a different challenge from the pips. At the start of the 20th century the numbered suit cards remained an empty field, with virtually no symbolic imagery at all. The courts, however, have always shown actual characters. Unfortunately, the characters pose in such formal portraits that they convey very little meaning.

the court cards

Because of the need to open up the courts, this section of the deck has ended up with some of the greatest variety in imagery. Even the names have changed. The Golden Dawn deck began it with King, Queen, Prince, and Princess. Various modern decks have substituted the idea of a family – Mother, Father, Son, and Daughter. Others have suggested spiritual traditions from other cultures with such titles as Shaman, Priestess, Chief, Warrior, Amazon, and so on. And some Tarots have portrayed the stages of individual development, as in the Voyager's Child, Man, Woman, and Sage.

Because of the great variety in pictures we will follow six decks through this section.

tarot de marseilles

This is the classic version. The formal pictures of the Tarot de Marseilles give few overt clues to the cards' meanings. A closer look at the cards, however, will show the subtle differences in character and symbolism.

Queen of Coins, Tarot de Marseilles. The classic style gives little clue to the card's meaning.

KING of PENTACLES.

King of Pentacles, Universal Waite Tarot. The face and body posture hint at the card's qualities.

PRINCE OF CUPS

Prince of Cups, Golden Dawn Tarot.

Like the Marseilles, the figures pose formally. They do, however, give more hints to their meaning, especially in the Pages and Knights. Notice, for example, the postures and expressions on the Pages, and what they do with their suit emblems. With the Knights, look at the horses, how the Wands rears, the Cups hardly moves, the Swords gallops, and the Pentacles stands still, as if planted. With the Kings and Queens we can read their expressions and the way they sit, for example the grimness of the Queen of Swords, or the fond way the King of Pentacles strokes his golden disk. Animal imagery also gives us clues to their meaning (see The Tarot Bestiary, page 127).

the golden dawn

Mathers' deck brought sexual balance to the court cards by changing the male Knight and Page to Prince and Princess, a change that also introduced the notion of generations, that is, the King and Queen join together in order to produce the Prince and Princess. The deck extends the Marseilles pictures in another way, by having the characters act in symbolic and sometimes dramatic ways, such as the Queen of Swords, with her severed head. The Hermetic Order developed the idea of linking both positions and suits to elements. Kings represent Fire, Queens become Water, and Prince and Princess Air and Earth. Each card thus becomes a combination. The King of Cups, for example, is Fire of Water. Many modern decks have used this system.

In her striking pictures, Frieda Harris extended symbolism through the power of art. Aleister Crowley's titles also extended the Golden Dawn ideas by changing the King to a Knight. The change produces a storyline. The wandering Knight courts the Queen. She takes him as her consort, and they give birth to the Prince and Princess. This story goes back to a medieval tradition called courtly love, in which a knight serves his lady. Courtly love may have come from the same roots as the Albigensian heresy, one possible source for the Tarot itself.

A number of modern decks have used the court cards as a mythological gallery. Haindl has done this more systematically than most, choosing a different culture – and continent – for each suit. Haindl made his choices symbolically. Cups meant the Holy Grail, and therefore Europe, in the North. West to him meant the Native Americans. Since he saw this culture as close to the Earth, that meant the suit of Stones. East meant India, but also the dawn and therefore Fire, and so Wands. This left Swords for the South. Haindl chose Egypt to represent Africa. He painted each suit in the artistic style of its people.

Queen of Cups, Thoth Tarot.

Son of Stones in the West
Prince of Stones

Son of Stones in the West, Haindl Tarot. This deck draws on traditional cultures of four continents.

[the court cards] 243

The Voyager Tarot was conceived by James Wanless and Ken Knutson in the 1980s. This deck represents two strands in modern Tarot – the use of collage to evoke the inner quality of the card, and the choice of titles that show the stages of a human life rather than social positions in society.

Man of Wands, Voyager Tarot.

Prince of Swords, Golden Dawn. The Order linked this card to the Air element.

THE PAGES

The usual approach to the court cards is that they represent character types. In readings, we often think of them as specific people, and the particular card, with its special characteristics, will help us identify just which person it is.

Even the Golden Dawn text (quoted by Robert Wang in his *An Introduction to the Golden Dawn Tarot*), which says things like "The Princesses rule over the four parts of the Celestial Heavens which lie around the North Pole," will describe a specific card (Princess of Wands) as "Brilliance, courage, sudden in anger or love …" Whether as Page, Valet, Knave, Princess, Daughter, or Child, this card signifies someone young – at least young in spirit if not in actual years. These people may be students, or people who are trying something new in life. What they all share is an eagerness and a fresh attitude toward life itself.

In readings about the family, or for a woman who wants to become pregnant, a Page card can refer to an actual child or a baby. However, these cards also can reveal states of mind.

The variety of decks available show us the ways in which different people have elaborated these concepts.

The Marseilles shows young men, quiet and contemplative compared to the Knights. The Waite gives us gentle figures

Page of Cups, Tarot de Marseilles. The Pages symbolize someone young, whether in age or in spirit.

at ease with their suit emblems. By contrast, the Golden Dawn emphasizes eagerness and energy in its pictures of bare-breasted Amazons who bring the power of the suit to life (the Order joined the Princesses to the last letter of God's name, the point at which the process of creation comes to reality). The Thoth shows active figures as well, amid swirling energy. The Voyager portrays particular qualities of children, appropriate to their elements – Seeker for Fiery Wands, Feeler for Cups Water, Learner for the Mental Crystals (Swords), and Learner for Worlds (Pentacles), the suit of Earth.

The fact that some decks show a male Page or Knave, while others show a Princess, reminds us that the court cards are not actually gender-linked. They are defined by personality and actions. This is especially true for the Pages.

Child of Cups, Voyager Tarot.

The Suits

The character and the suit go together well. Even if we think of the Princess as Earth, she still expresses the idea of a fresh beginning. The Page of Wands is eager, excited, and ready to try new things. She or he can be a very loyal friend or lover, for there is no duplicity in this person. The Haindl character, Radha *(right),* emphasizes playfulness and a love of life.

When we reverse a court card, the pure character encounters outside pressure. In this situation the simple Page can become indecisive, even confused, as life seems too complex at times. Reversed, this card may also symbolize unfaithfullness.

Daughter of Wands in the East
Princess of Wands

page of cups

The Waite gives us a wonderful picture of a dreamy person who can look at thoughts and fantasies without feeling any pressure to act on them. The Page can signify psychic development. The Voyager Child feels life very directly, while Haindl's Brigid shows someone who is calm and serene.

Reversed, the Page confuses fantasy with reality and the person may act on impulse, for instance buying something unnecessary just to fulfill a fantasy, or making promises without intentions of keeping them, or pursuing an unrequited love.

Page of Cups, Universal Waite Tarot.

This Page is alert and vigilant, a person quick and intelligent. In the Haindl, Isis is one of the strongest cards, a goddess whose strong will and dedication overcome all opposition. She does not triumph through violence but through courage and love. The Voyager Child of Crystals explores the wonders of the mind, while the Golden Dawn and Thoth Princesses stress subtlety and grace.

Reversed, the Page's vigilance can turn to anxiety, even paranoia. He may also suffer from a loss of confidence.

Left
Page of Swords, Universal Waite Tarot.

Right
Princess of Swords, Thoth Tarot.

PAGE of SWORDS.

Princess of Swords

The Waite shows an ideal student, so caught up in his Pentacle he seems to notice nothing else. The Haindl shifts this to a teacher, for White Buffalo Woman came to give sacred knowledge to the Lakota. The Voyager emphasizes play. What connects all these approaches is the idea of someone who immerses himself in the world in all its wonder.

Reversed, the Page is easily distracted. He follows every impulse or whim rather than focus energy or purpose. Play becomes an excuse to avoid responsibility.

Left
Page of Pentacles, Universal Waite Tarot.

Right
Child of Worlds, Voyager Tarot.

THE KNIGHTS

Knight of Wands, Tarot de Marseilles. The Knights are idealistic figures, who go on quests for the good of mankind.

Knight of Wands, Universal Waite Tarot.

KNIGHT of WANDS.

When we move from the Page to the Knight we find a new complexity. Between a child and an adult, the Knights combine eager energy and responsibility. Knights ride into the world to test themselves and seek adventures. And yet, they also must act for the good of others. They do not go on quests just for their own gain but to aid the helpless. This gives them an idealistic quality but it may put them at odds with the youthful desire for self-discovery.

Moreover, the suit may also work against the character of the Knight. While Wands and Swords go well with this character, dreamy Cups and hard-working Pentacles can conflict with the Knight's high energy and risk-taking.

The Marseilles' Cavaliers all appear rather stately, as if on parade. The Golden Dawn's Princes pose like the Marseilles but these Princes are in their chariots, symbols of activity. As the older child of the King and Queen, the Prince extends and uses their primal powers. The Thoth deck uses chariots as well, and makes them dynamic to give a sense of action.

The Haindl Sons emphasize knightly responsibility. Each of the Knights accepts that his main purpose is to serve the world in some altruistic way. Parsifal (Cups) looks with horror at a vision of what his ancestors have done and the need to change the world. Krishna (Wands) maintains Fire joy and sensuality while still leading people to enlightenment. Osiris (Swords) grants new life to the dead, while Seattle (Stones) was an actual historical person who lectured the United States Congress on its responsibility to the Earth.

The Voyager deck presents the many ways in which men explore and learn their roles in life. The Wands Actor card shows us the different kinds of performances that men undertake. The Man of Cups Surfer card shows the masculine love of thrills. The Man of Crystals Inventor and Man of Worlds Achiever cards deal with humankind's many and varied accomplishments, as well as various different careers.

The Suits

knight of wands

Someone adventurous and energetic. He is eager to experience life, eager to see the world and experiment. He can be very helpful, chivalrous in fact, as long as nobody tries to hold him back or control him. This card may indicate travel or some kind of new experience. As a lover, he may be attractive but not necessarily loyal.

Reversed, he meets setbacks and opposition. His confidence gets shaken as he makes mistakes. However, his natural optimism means that nothing will stop him for long. The reversed Knight of Wands may mean delays in a project.

Son of Wands in the West. Haindl Tarot.

Son of Wands in the East.
Prince of Wands

Whether in the Waite version, half lost in his vision (see also the Thoth, who stares into his Cup even as his chariot pulls him along), or the Haindl Parsifal who does not want to acknowledge what he sees, this Knight faces a conflict. Cups symbolize dreams, imagination, and vision, not action. In relationships, this Knight may indicate someone drawn to romance but reluctant to get involved, or to share his inner emotions.

Reversed, the world – relationships, job, family – puts pressure on him to give up his dreams and become more active. He may resent these demands.

Left
Knight of Cups, Universal Waite Tarot.

Right
Son of Cups in the North, Haindl Tarot.

KNIGHT of CUPS.

PARSIVAL

Son of Cups in the North
Prince of Cups

He is the bravest of the Knights, for after all the Sword is the Knight's tool. In the Thoth, we see the Prince about to wield his Sword in the abstract realm of the mind. The Rider emphasizes the more mundane image of a Knight who charges into a storm. Nothing will stop him. In the Waite picture, the horse looks frightened, almost as if doubting the wisdom of the Knight's desire to charge. The Voyager also lets nothing stop him as he tries out one experiment after another.

Reversed, his bravery becomes foolhardiness, or even aggression. He is quick to attack but finds it harder to listen.

Left
Knight of Swords, Universal Waite Tarot.

Right
Prince of Swords, Thoth Tarot.

Like the Cups Knight, he does not fit comfortably with his suit. Even the Voyager Man of Worlds, with his corporate success and Rolls-Royce and runner's trophy, may long for the freedom just to take off and try new things. The Haindl Son is the exception, for he has fully accepted his responsibility for the world around him.

The Waite figure sits on a stationary horse. This character is hard-working, responsible, and uncomplaining.

Reversed, he may resent the lack of excitement in his life. Or he may suddenly lose the work that has claimed all his attention.

Left
Knight of Pentacles, Universal Waite Tarot.

Right
Man of Worlds, Voyager Tarot.

KNIGHT of PENTACLES

THE QUEENS

With the Queens and Kings we come to the mature expressions of the suit. These characters know who they are, and they know their rightful place in the world.

We usually look for a woman in our lives when one of the Queen cards shows up in our Tarot reading. If we are female, we might think of ourselves and consider our role as a wife or a mother. Or we might think of the ways in which we express power in our lives. Alternatively, we might think of someone that we know.

Actually, the Queens express a quality as much as the female gender. That quality is appreciation of life. The Queens inspire rather than command.

The Queens of the Marseilles Tarot deck sit on their throne and ponder the emblems of their power. That is, all except for the Queen of Wands, who looks out with that Wands' eagerness. The Queen of Wands is the only Queen to sit with her legs apart, a sexual posture that we find also in the Waite. While the suit of Cups rules love, the suit of Wands rules desire.

The Alchemical Queen of Coins holds a cornucopia as well as her suit emblem.

Queen of Wands, Universal Waite Tarot.

Mother of Wands in the East, depicting Kali, Haindl Tarot.

The Golden Dawn Queens look at their emblem of power, aware of its strength. Animals attend three of them. The fourth, Swords, holds that severed head. We might think of it as anyone foolish enough to try to control her. Alternatively, we might consider it the ego, with the Queen a symbol of mental courage.

The Queens of the Thoth Tarot deck borrow imagery from the Golden Dawn deck (including the severed head) but these Queens immerse themselves more powerfully in their element.

The Haindl Mothers are the most powerful in the suit. They are ancient, life-giving, the source, as well as the wielders, of great power. And yet, they are never aggressive, not even the Hindu goddess Kali, fearsome as she is, for they do not need to prove anything.

The Women of the Voyager deck express a firmness about their place in the world. We see intense experience in the Wands and Cups – Sensor and Rejoicer, and a nurturing and love in Crystals and Worlds – Guardian and Preserver.

The Suits

queen of wands

Confident, powerful, radiant with Sun Fire, this leonine Queen attracts admirers by her love of life, her warmth, and possibly her sexuality. She also can overwhelm people at times (as we see in Kali), especially those who lack her great self-confidence, or who find life difficult and frightening. She may need to add compassion to her confidence.

Reversed, the Queen confronts adversity and suffering. Her first reaction is to tackle the problem, or help others in trouble. If it goes on too long, she may just want to leave.

queen of cups

This is a very intense card, for Water is the most feminine of suits. The Golden Dawn calls this card Water of Water. The Haindl Mother of Cups is the most mysterious but also the oldest. This figurine is the oldest known human sculpture, at 35,000 years of age. We see the same power in the Voyager Rejoicer, the power of love and sensuality. The Waite Queen looks intently at her elaborate Cup. Though she sits firmly on land (reality), the steam (emotions) flows into her dress. She is the Queen of love.

Reversed, her creative forceful personality may lose its creative purpose. She may become aggressive or untrustworthy.

Mother of Cups in the North, Haindl Tarot.

Queen of Cups, Golden Dawn Tarot.

If Cups is love, the Swords Queen is the Queen of sorrow. The Waite picture shows her sitting high on a hill, alone. She may be a woman (or man) alone, possibly a widow. But she is not downcast, or feeling sorry for herself. Above all, she believes in the truth. Her Sword points straight up, like the sword of justice. Other versions stress her powerful mind and her total honesty to others as well as herself.

Reversed, she may indeed give way to self-pity. The reversed Queen also may become narrow-minded or manipulative.

Left
Queen of Swords, Universal Waite Tarot.

Right
Mother of Swords in the South, Haindl Tarot.

QUEEN of SWORDS

Mother of Swords in the South
Queen of Swords

This is a lush card. The Queen of Earth is a Queen of prosperity and fertility. The Voyager Woman of Worlds is pregnant, while the Waite sits in an abundant garden. She holds her pentacle in both hands and looks down with an awareness of all the good things life has given her. Her physical surroundings matter greatly to her, whether in nature or a beautiful home. She believes in herself and shares her wealth and happiness freely.

Reversed, she loses her important connection to the simple things in life. As a result, she can doubt herself and find it difficult to function.

Left
Queen of Pentacles, Universal Waite Tarot.

Right
Woman of Worlds, Voyager Tarot.

THE KINGS

The final card in the suit brings us to wisdom and maturity, but also responsibility. The traditional position of a King requires him to make decisions for the greater good. A King in a reading may signify someone in charge, someone who has achieved mastery in his field, usually an older man.

The traditional role of the King requires him to make decisions for the good of others.

The Voyager Sages show the fullness of the elemental energy. The Seer (Wands) finds power and knowledge in the Fire of creation while the Regenerator (Cups) understands and uses the life-giving Waters that flow through all existence. The Knower (Crystals) shows us Einstein peering into the abstract structures of the universe. And the Master (Worlds) understands the most complex of all realities, daily life.

The Marseilles cards give us a mix of characters. The two active suits, Wands and Swords, portray young men, clean-shaven and energetic. The more settled Cups and Coins portray old men with beards. The King of Coins wears no crown, for he represents the merchant class. The King of Swords wears face-plates on his shoulders like those on the trump card, the Charioteer.

The Thoth cards confuse us slightly by replacing the King with the Knight as the Queen's partner. They are making explicit an idea from the Golden Dawn, who depict the four Kings on horseback, riding forth with the emblem of their power. The Thoth deck shows swift movement in all but the Knight of Disks, who draws energy from the Earth.

In the Golden Dawn and Thoth systems, the King/Knight embodies *yod,* the first letter of God's name and the spark of Fire energy that awakens the Queen's Water power. Their symbolic union goes back thousands of years, to all those cultures (from Sumeria to Ireland) where the king married the goddess of the land in a ritual act to promote fertility.

We find a similar idea in the Haindl deck, where the Mothers actually signify the oldest expression of human culture and religion. The Fathers show the stage at which humanity codifies its customs in law.

Unlike its Golden Dawn predecessors, the Waite shows us genuine rulers. Among other things, the four Kings give us the ways that people react to responsibility and power.

King of Swords, Tarot de Marseilles. This young figure wears a hat rather than a crown.

The Suits

The King of Fire is strong-willed, with supreme belief in his own power. He may be flamboyant and very attractive, a natural leader, sexual and charismatic. He also may be intolerant of weakness or of other people's doubts and fears.

Reversed, life gives him setbacks. As a result he may become more compassionate and understanding, as well as more serious and austere.

Left
Father of Wands, Haindl Tarot.

Right
King of Wands, Golden Dawn Tarot.

Father of Stones in the West
King of Stones

KING OF WANDS

Emotions and artistic inspiration, like water, change and flow. Such subtleties do not go well with the King's need to be in charge and care for others. While this card may mean someone successful in the arts, it more often will indicate someone who controls his emotions, or who channels artistic interests into work that will bring him commercial success.

Reversed can mean an outburst of suppressed emotion. It also may mean someone who takes a risk to pursue a dream.

Left
King of Cups, Universal Waite Tarot.

Right
King of Cups, Golden Dawn Tarot.

KING of CUPS.

KING OF CUPS

One of the most powerful of the court cards. Kingly authority matches the Swords themes of intellect, judgment, and force. The card signifies someone strong-minded, even brilliant. He may overwhelm people who do not think as clearly and brilliantly as he does. At his best he is idealistic and fair. He may, however, see things from a narrow rationalist perspective, with little respect for emotions.

Reversed, he may misuse his intellectual power to dominate or gain advantage. However, it also can signify self-doubt, or a willingness to listen to others' opinions.

Left
King of Swords, Universal Waite Tarot.

Right
Knight of Swords, Thoth Tarot. Crowley made the Knights mature figures rather than Kings.

He is possibly the happiest of the Kings, for he enjoys his success, his wealth, and his good life. He likes being the boss and takes pride in his accomplishments and the loyalty of those around him. He also enjoys the material trappings of success. Notice the way the Waite King looks fondly at his Pentacle, the way he sits comfortably on his throne.

Reversed, some kind of setback or loss makes him question himself. Without his outer achievements to justify his life he may think of himself as a failure.

Left
King of Pentacles, Golden Dawn Tarot.

Right
King of Pentacles, Universal Waite Tarot.

KING OF PENTACLES

KING of PENTACLES

PART FOUR

readings

No matter how much we study, memorize, or look things up, when we set out the cards for a reading we confront them in their most direct form — there is no dodging their intense messages. And no matter how many times we have witnessed the cards' amazing ability to reach into our lives and the lives of others, every time is like the first time. As we mix the cards, we cannot help but wonder what we will discover, what flash of revelation will come as we stare at the vivid pictures. Will the cards reveal long-buried secrets? Will they guide us to a better future? Or maybe help us understand the past? Remember that the Tarot always works for our benefit. Any divination system will tell us something. The Tarot tells us things that open our understanding because the Tarot is a book of wisdom, a model for the growth of the soul. Think of a Tarot reader. What do you see? An elderly woman in a dark room with a black candle burning beside her worn and faded cards? Or maybe an innocent teenager telling fortunes at a party who gasps as she turns over Death or some other fearful card. Or do you see yourself?

When most people think about Tarot they think of readings. And often, what they think is tinged with fear. Ask them if they want a reading and they may laugh, embarrassed, and say "No thanks, that stuff scares me." Or they may have tried reading cards themselves when they were younger, but then put them away when they discovered it worked. Partly the images scare people, all those men with swords in their backs, the Devil with his chained slaves, and Death harvesting heads. Or maybe they heard somewhere that Tarot is evil, involved with "black magic."

Mostly, however, what scares people about Tarot is the idea that it works. How could such a thing be? How can you mix a pack of cards, choose some at random, and discover things about yourself or others – let alone predict future events? And how can a total stranger do such things? No wonder it scares people.

We can justify astrology to ourselves by the mightiness of the stars and planets. To many people it makes sense that celestial objects so much bigger than we are should influence events. Doesn't gravity affect the Earth? And the stars and planets change position over time according to strict mathematical laws. The fall of Tarot cards seems totally random, and, if you mix the deck again and do a second reading, you will get different cards. The fact is, our very smallness makes the effect of gravity extremely slight (other forces, such as electricity, or the energy in our atoms, affect us much more directly), and the planets do not actually enter and leave the constellations at the time and dates written on our calendars or in astrological ephemerides (the constellations move very slowly, but they do move). Astrology, like Tarot, functions primarily as an organized way to create a symbolic pattern and system.

All divination works through patterns. Divination makes an assumption, that the patterns we create through

The Tarot's reputation for black magic comes from simple ignorance of its genuine spiritual message.

mixing different bits of information will tell us something meaningful about our lives. In the case of astrology, the bits of information involve the planets and signs as they move in relation to each other according to mathematical formulas. In the case of Tarot, the information involves the symbolic meanings of 78 picture cards shuffled together and laid out according to a series of questions.

How does it work? The simple answer is that nobody knows. In ancient times, people believed that the gods or spirits directly influenced the fall of the cards, so that they would give a true answer. Remember that "divination" comes from "divine." Modern people who find such an idea

Carl Jung (1875–1961), the Swiss psychiatrist, who introduced the term synchronicity.

Synchronicity

The term synchronicity, invented by the psychologist C. G. Jung and the physicist Wolfgang Pauli, describes the idea that an "acausal principle" connects events just as cause and effect connects them. When we create a random pattern – by mixing cards without looking at the pictures – we allow this principle to emerge. Another way of looking at this is to say that a kind of invisible web ties together all existence, including the past and future, and that by creating a small web of images we mirror the larger web of our experience.

Do readings work?

We might ask all those people who tried it as a joke and became scared. As a beginning reader, you may discover such things as which of your neighbors are having affairs, or what will happen in business deals. However, do not expect infallibility or constant revelations. Sometimes the cards simply will not click for a person. Or they may tell us a great deal but we do not know how to understand them, not until after events and we look back at the reading and say "Oh, of course. That's what they meant. It's so obvious. Why didn't I see that?" So by all means try it. But beware, especially at the beginning, of taking yourself, and the cards, too seriously.

And beware too of any idea that the cards create events, or force anything to happen. Nothing in the Tarot or any other divination system can make you or anyone else do something you would not otherwise do, or act against your nature in any way. The cards illuminate. They do not create events.

The cards cannot cause events to occur. They merely illuminate past, present, or future events.

uncomfortable will sometimes invoke a concept called "synchronicity" *(see box)*. But even though this all sounds more scientific, it really just begs the question, how do readings work? Nobody knows.

FREE WILL AND OTHER QUESTIONS

Sometimes people wonder, if the cards indeed show us what will happen, does that mean we can never change anything? Must we surrender to what they say? Remember first of all that even the most experienced reader will sometimes miss an important aspect, or simply misinterpret something. We must always take our readings with a trace of scepticism based on our own fallibility. Many readers write down their readings, for themselves and others, just so they can look back on them later and see what they missed. This way they learn and at the same time they keep their humility.

But even if we could read Tarot cards with absolute precision they still would not show us fixed events. They show patterns and likelihoods. They tell us "This is the way things look at this moment. Given these people, and these situations, such and such events will likely occur."

Ideally, any Tarot reading should increase free will, not diminish it. This is because readings teach us about ourselves, and the issues facing us. The more information we have, the easier it becomes to change a direction, head off a problem, or help some wonderful development come into reality. The modern Tarot revival has always sought to empower people, to give them the tools to change themselves and their lives. To this end, many readers focus on issues in the person's life rather than predictions. Instead

If you write your readings down and return to them later you may find they mean even more after a few weeks than when you first laid them out.

of asking "When will Mark find a partner?" the reader might suggest that Mark use the cards to help him understand what is keeping him from finding someone. If a person goes to a reader to ask, "Will my husband leave his new girlfriend and return to me?" (a not uncommon question), the reader might try to answer the question but then go on to help the questioner recognize what she might do with her life besides wait for her errant husband to come home.

At one extreme stands the person who says, "The cards predict it, there's nothing I can do." At the other we find the attitude, "Now that I've seen where all the problems lie I

A Tarot reading is a partnership between the questioner, the reader, and the cards. All three contribute to the knowledge gained.

The cards endeavor to teach us about ourselves and the challenges that face us.

can make sure to avoid them." Avoiding problems may not be as easy as it seems. We are all the product of many forces, including desire, conditioning, a lifetime of habits, and circumstances beyond our control. Some of our habits serve us well, some do not. Some of our desires may bring us trouble. And even if we recognize our conditioned behavior we still need to change it. A good Tarot reading gives us information. It does not live our lives for us.

Many Tarot readers will refuse to answer questions about the behavior or emotions of someone other than the "querent" (the person who is seeking the reading). For one thing, they may consider that it is an invasion of privacy to uncover someone's private feelings or intentions without that person's knowledge. They also may doubt the accuracy of the information they get, since it may take on the hopes and attitudes of the person who is actually mixing the cards.

And yet, many people will go to a Tarot reader for just this reason – to find out if their partner loves them, or is faithful, or if their boss will give them a raise. In such cases, a reader may help the querent look at the question in ways that will put the focus more on them. Instead of asking, "Does Margaret love me?" the question might become, "What do I get out of my relationship with Margaret?" Instead of, "Will my boss promote me?" the querent might ask, "How can I improve my chances for a promotion?"

Psychic powers

You do not need psychic powers to read Tarot cards. If
you do possess such talent, work with the cards will
likely bring it out. Many people, however, do very well
with Tarot without ever looking for psychic flashes. They
interpret the cards through their knowledge of the
symbols joined to an intuitive sense of what the cards
are trying to say. We always need intuition, for each
card offers many possibilities and we need to trust an
inner sense of which one applies. Such intuition,
however, does not demand psychic power. It simply
comes with practice.

If you are blessed with psychic
powers, Tarot will help to bring
out such a talent. However, it
is not necessary to have
psychic powers to do a
reading, intuition is all that is
needed.

FREQUENTLY ASKED QUESTIONS

Many beliefs and stereotypes have grown up around Tarot readings. People may think the cards contain magic powers all by themselves and fear letting the cards into their homes. As Tarot writer Mary K. Greer once commented, Tarot cards are four-color pictures printed on cardboard. The magic lies within ourselves. Nor can the cards miraculously predict the future down to minute details. If they did, every Tarot reader would become a millionaire from stock investments and horse races. What the cards can do is illuminate ourselves and our predicaments. Moreover, they give us tools to change the only area that we really can control – ourselves.

The cards themselves are not magical, but working with their teachings can raise us to a higher level.

Here are some common questions and answers about the cards:

"Can I buy my own deck?" Somehow the legend has grown up that someone else, preferably an old Gypsy woman, must give you your Tarot cards. Some people have waited for years to begin reading cards because no mysterious figure appeared to give them a deck. If we really needed this to happen, the publishers of Tarot decks would soon go out of business. Again, the magic does not lie in the cards, or in strangers, but in yourself. If you really do not feel comfortable buying your own deck, choose the one you want and ask a friend or relative to give it to you for your birthday.

"How do I choose a deck?" There are literally hundreds of decks available. Though they come sealed, stores will often carry samples to give you a sense of the art and the themes. But how to make a choice? Many people prefer to begin with the Rider-Waite-Smith, with its vivid action scenes and consistent symbolism. Others prefer the Crowley-Harris Thoth deck for the beauty of its art and its complexity and daring themes, or the traditionalism of the Tarot de Marseilles, or the antiquity of the Visconti. And there are those who like the contemporary look of the Voyager, or the goddess tradition of the Motherpeace. You will probably find that the deck that attracts you the most is the one that works best for you. However, if you work with it for a while and find that you still like it but cannot connect with it, go back and find another.

Top
The Magician from the Cary-Yale Visconti Tarot.

Above
Haindl's conception of the Magician card.

Below
The Motherpeace Tarot Magician.

The Magician from Tarot de Marseilles.

The Magician, Thoth Tarot.

"Can I use more than one deck?" Some people use different decks for different kinds of readings and others for esoteric study or meditation. However, many people find that they can learn better with a single deck and branch out later. "Can I allow others to touch my cards?" Some people want only their own energy to enter the cards. If you feel this way, honor it. It will mean you must shuffle the cards yourself, but you can bring the querent into it through some ritual action, such as having the person place a hand on either side of the deck before you mix it. At the same time, most readers prefer the querent to shuffle the cards directly. What does matter to many people is that they take their cards seriously, which means they do not pass them around at parties or let people play with them. Some readers keep a duplicate deck just to show friends and use their main deck only for readings.

"Do I need to wrap them in silk?" Tradition says we should protect our cards from "psychic contamination" in a silk scarf when not in use. Whether or not you believe this, a beautiful scarf will help honor the Tarot and the importance of its place in your life. You may want to spread the scarf on the table and lay the cards on top of it when you do your readings.

Skill and practice

"Do I need to memorize all the meanings before I can start?" There are two extremes among Tarot readers. One group believes you should ignore anything written about the cards, including the meanings given by the deck's creator, and only follow your instincts. Though this works for some people it ignores both the deliberate meanings coded into the pictures, and the centuries of wisdom that have grown up around them.

Tarot readings acquire greater depth of meaning over time.

The other extreme says we must memorize everything in the instruction book before we attempt our first reading. Tarot reading is a skill, and as with any skill we learn best through practice. There is no harm in laying down a card and then checking the book for what it might mean. Even experienced readers will benefit now and then from referring to their books, for all of us will lock into favorite interpretations and forget other possibilities.

Many people have questions about the relationship between the reader and the querent. The first question wonders whether you need two people – "Can I read for myself?"

the reader and the querent

Tarot myth says you must never read for yourself. No one knows the origin of this notion, but no such ban exists and no danger will come to you if you read your own cards. An old adage claims that a lawyer who represents himself has a fool for a client. The same may hold for Tarot but in the Tarot world a Fool is not such a bad thing to be. Some people only read for themselves, and Mary K. Greer has written a whole book on the subject, her popular *Tarot For Yourself.*

The only problem in reading your own cards lies in objectivity. Since most people want a Tarot reading in times of trouble, even anguish, you may find it hard to look at the cards in a truly calm manner and try to understand them the way you would for someone else. And you might get an instant reaction and not look any further, something you could not do if you were reading for a client or a friend. If you find it difficult to read your own cards you might talk about them out loud, as if you are talking to someone else. Or you might find a friend who also reads the cards and agree to a regular exchange of readings.

"Are there any rules?" Suppose you do want to read for others, even professionally. Do you need to make any rules

If you do readings for others, you should make it clear what you do and do not do.

with the people you see? This depends on you. You should make it clear, especially to people you don't know well, just what you do and do not do. If you use the cards to develop awareness and do not like to predict future events you should tell people. Similarly, if you know the person wants spiritual guidance on how to live his or her life, and you do not want to take on that role, you need to say so at the outset of the reading.

"Should I tell people what to do?" The signs in storefronts say "Tarot Reader and Adviser." Some readers see it as their duty to give direct advice. "Don't marry that man. He'll cheat on you." "Take the job at the bank. You'll rise quickly." After all, people have come to the reader for just this kind of information. If you can see such things, shouldn't you pass them on? And yet, other readers would never think to tell someone what to do. For them, the querent needs to make her or his own decisions and the reader should only help clarify the questions. As a Tarot reader, you need to decide this issue for yourself – though you may wish to ask your cards.

"Should I charge money for the readings I do?" Since many people make their living reading cards, they obviously feel comfortable asking for money. And yet, some people feel adamantly that the ability to help people comes as a gift

How you feel about charging (or paying) money for Tarot readings may tell you about your own relationship to money.

and they should not profit from it. They point to shamans and other traditional healers who do not charge for what they do. We should realize that in such cultures the entire village will support the shaman, with a home and food, and the individual people the shaman helps will give gifts. Our society functions on the giving and receiving of money. When a reader asks for money, he or she is saying, "I believe enough in what I do to ask people to give me something in return."

"Should the querents tell me their questions?" Once again, we are up against the fantasy of the magical Tarot reader. Sometimes, if you say to people, "What do you want the cards to look at?" they will answer, "You're the Tarot reader. You tell me." Now, some readers really do prefer the querent to say nothing. They want to deal only with the messages that come from the cards. And if the person doesn't tell you the issue, the cards very likely will make it clear, with pictures of romance, say, or conflicts at work. Often, however, this becomes a kind of parlor game. The reader guesses at the problem and the querent goes away impressed with the "accuracy" of the reading. But have they learned anything new? If the querent tells you the question right away, you can give your attention to answers and decisions. Gail Fairfield, who also wrote a book entitled *Tarot For Yourself*, puts it this way. If you go to a doctor and you are asked what your symptoms are you do not say, "You're the doctor. You tell me."

In societies such as the Aboriginal cultures of Australia, healers and diviners serve the whole community, which supports them in turn.

The first thing you need to do is mix the cards. Veteran card players tend to shuffle Tarot cards the way they do poker or canasta. There is one difference, however, with Tarot. If you use reversed meanings you will want the querent to mix the cards so that some of them get turned around.

getting started

One way to do this (also good for decks too large to shuffle in your hands) is to lay the deck on the table, face down of course, then spread them all around, like a child making a mud pie. This method also works if you want to do a spread for two people together, since they both can move the cards at the same time. When the querent has thoroughly mixed the cards, she or he brings the deck back together, then with the left hand cuts the deck into three piles. The reader, also with the left hand, places the bottom pile on top of the middle, and the two together on top of the first. *(See pages 288–9, where these steps are illustrated.)* Alternatively, some readers like to hold the left hand a little above each pile and sense which one radiates heat. We use the left hand for these activities to invoke intuition, for the left side of the human body subtly stresses wholeness and an intuitive grasp of situations. The right side emphasizes reason and the ability to explain. We use the right hand to turn over the cards for the reading.

Some people like to do a ritual, either before the shuffle or just before they look at the pictures. They may light a candle, or take a moment to close their eyes, breathe deeply, release extraneous thoughts and worries, and focus their attention properly on the cards. They may ask their guiding spirits to help them discover whatever truths will

Rituals, such as lighting a candle, may help to focus the mind before a reading.

help the querent. Or they may visualize particular cards that symbolize qualities they need for the reading, such as the High Priestess on the left and the Magician on the right. And some people, who practice Wicca or other ritual-based spirituality, may wish to do a more elaborate ritual, complete with magical tools and invocations to the four directions. None of this is strictly necessary. Those who do these things find it helps them give all their attention, psychic as well as conscious, to the cards and their message.

When we turn over the cards with our right hand, where do we place them? The answer lies in "spreads." A spread is a pattern in which each position carries a special value, such as "past events" and "near future," or "what blocks me" and "what helps me." Just as the meaning of a Minor Arcana card emerges from the combination of its number and its suit, so the actual message of a card combines the card itself and its place within the spread.

A simple example will make this clear. A recently divorced woman wants to know if she will find a new husband. She mixes the cards and the Lovers turns up. Obviously this means romance, but in what context? If "past experience," it refers to the genuine love she once knew, before the marriage turned bad. The cards would not tell her this just to remind her what she has lost, but rather to help her remember that she knows the power of love. Still, it remains in the past. If the position is "hope," it shows her desire. If "possible development," it says she may find someone later in life. But if the Lovers falls in "near future" or "outcome," it will answer her much more decisively.

Hundreds of spreads exist, possibly even thousands, since almost all Tarot readers make up new ones from time to time. Some recent Tarot books consist almost entirely of different spreads, from the simplest to spreads that use the entire deck and look at the person's whole life, even spreads from past and future lives. Spreads often address special issues, such as work, or relationships.

You do not actually use spreads to read Tarot cards. Some people prefer to turn the cards over and let the images trigger responses. Other people like to construct a spread just for that querent and her or his questions. We see how to do this, including possible questions on the following pages. Most readers, however, especially beginners, like the direction of a definite spread.

Step 2
After bringing the cards back together, the querent
should use the left hand to cut the deck into three

Step 1
The deck should be spread around and the cards
mixed up thoroughly. This will ensure that some of the
cards will become reversed.

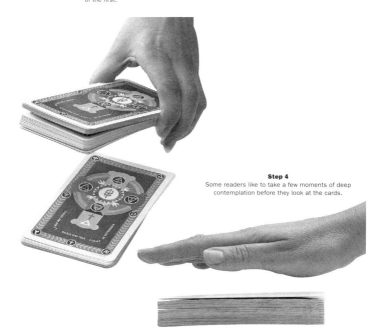

Step 3
Again with the left hand, the reader places the bottom pile on top of the middle, and the two together on top of the first.

Step 4
Some readers like to take a few moments of deep contemplation before they look at the cards.

Can a single card constitute a spread? It can if the "position" has a meaning. The most common meanings are "guidance for today" or "what I need to look at today" or "what will help me today."

In other words, people choose a card each morning to help them understand what they will be facing over the next 24 hours. This practice may sound a little obsessive, as if the person cannot do anything without checking their card. In reality, however, it often helps to take some of the nervousness out of the more fearsome images, such as the Tower, or some of the Swords cards. You may get the Ten of Swords one morning and discover a lot of minor annoyances, and then the next day get the Four of Wands and notice a relief.

Some people choose a card a day when they get a new deck. Instead of sitting down and studying the deck like a college assignment, they get to learn it in action, like meeting a new friend.

To that purpose we will look at single cards from a pair of recent decks. The first is the Transformational Tarot by Arnell Ando, a carefully constructed collage Tarot deck that draws on the art of many traditions, mixed with popular culture. The chosen card is the Nine of Pentacles. The picture derives from the Waite image of the woman with the falcon sitting on her wrist. As a card for the day it suggests spending some part of the day in contemplation, with an emphasis on beauty. The person may want to dress in something special, take a little extra

If chosen as a card for the day, the Nine of Pentacles from the Transformational Tarot might suggest spending time quietly in nature.

Strength

Strength, from the Greenwood Tarot. People who get this card might want to visualize themselves as this magical lion-warrior.

care with esthetics, and take time out that day to see the wonder in nature.

The second deck is the Greenwood Tarot of Chesca Potter and Mark Ryan. Potter's striking art emphasizes the ancient roots of shamanic magic in the natural world. This time the card is Strength. Instead of the traditional image of a woman taming a lion, this version combines the two in the figure of a lion-headed hunter. The androgynous hunter holds a bloodied spear but also a cup filled with light, symbol of generosity. When we look at the book that comes with the deck, we will find that the card emphasizes the inner strength that is needed to face some longstanding problem. The person needs courage, even fierceness. As a card for the day it suggests an awareness of those special qualities as well as whatever problem may have bothered the person for a long time. Because it is a day card, moreover, it allows the person to touch his or her inner strength in a simple yet committed way.

Two cards seem a less popular number for spreads. This is largely because most things that you can do with two cards you also can do with three, and you can use the card in the middle to balance the other two cards (remember the Kabbalistic Tree of Life, where the middle pillar holds together the right and left sides).

The most obvious two-card spreads involve choices between two options. Any time we face two clear options we can choose a card for each to see what they might offer us. Such choices can range from whether to stay home or go to relatives for Christmas, to which of two offers of employment to accept. Although we should never base important decisions solely on the cards, they can help us to consider the issues, and they will, therefore, make our important decisions that much easier.

Think of a woman who must choose between two men. Both want a serious relationship with her and she knows that she cannot continue to see both, but must decide. However, a card for each could help her look at their different qualities and imagine the kind of life she might have with either man.

The first card is the Ten of Pentacles. The querent would find security with this man, but maybe also dullness. The second is the Knight of Wands. This card shows an adventurer, someone exciting, a risk taker. And yet, he may care more about those adventures than about her or their marriage. Notice that the cards do not say to choose one man or the other. Instead, they help the querent to see what might happen. She needs to compare these two images with her inner sense of the two men.

Often a reading will help us acknowledge what we already know. Now that the two cards have given her a kind of snapshot of the situation, she might want to try a more complete reading, one that would also look at the querent's own contributions to each of the relationships.

You may wish to use a simple two-card spread to help you choose between the two men in your life.

We looked earlier at the importance of the number three, in mythology with all the triple gods and goddesses, and in nature, especially the essential family unit of mother, father, and child. Maybe because of this significance, there are many three-card spreads in Tarot reading. Here are some of the more well known.

three-card readings

1. past, present, future

Lay the cards out 1, 2, 3. The first shows some experience in the past that has helped shape the current situation. The second describes what is going on right now. The third card shows where the person is heading. This does not mean a hard and fast prediction, though some people will read it that way. Instead, it offers a picture of what will likely happen, and why.

The Three Graces from Botticelli's *Primavera*. Three expresses a natural rhythm of life.

The simplicity of three cards can mask whole worlds of meaning.

The first card indicates a person's intellectual attitude. The second shows the person's actions. The reader might want to point out any contradictions between the two. For example, if the Mind card indicates anger (Swords or Wands or the Tower) while the body card shows the person accepting burdens (Ten of Wands) or expressing love (various Cups cards, the Lovers, or the Empress), then the person is swallowing all the anger. The third card, Spirit, indicates a lesson that the person can learn from the situation.

In this spread we see conflict as the middle, with possible approaches to the problem on either side.

Here we put down the middle card first, with the others on either side (2,1,3). The middle one describes the situation. The others indicate different ways the person can handle the central issue. Some people like to add another row below the first. Here the middle card indicates how the situation will likely develop if the person does not actively change it. The cards on either side of the middle card reflect the result of the two choices.

Here too we lay the cards 2, 1, 3, and the middle card shows a situation. In this case it describes a relationship. Card 2, on the left, reveals what the person has contributed to the situation. Card 3, on the right, shows the other person's behavior. This kind of reading can be very helpful for people in conflict. It can clarify what actually is going on, and more importantly, it can help prevent the querent from blaming either the other person or herself for the entire problem.

5. mother, father, child

We can use these designations literally, to show the relationships within a family.

In that case, a further card, placed above or below the row, can say something about the family as a whole. We also can use these titles as symbols. "Mother" indicates what nurtures the person, "Father" what teaches or disciplines. "Child" describes what the person experiences as a result of these forces.

Some people worry about the sexism of such formulas as "mother equals nurture and father equals discipline." The reading in the box, which used cards from the Wheel of Change Tarot, shows how the actual practice of Tarot reading can cut across such roles.

Mother, father, child reading

This reading concerned a man who sought ways to handle a time of great stress. The Mother card is the Knight of Disks. Right away we see the idea that a male image can symbolize what a querent needs as his "mother." The picture shows an Aztec warrior from ancient Mexico, and bears the subtitle (in the book for the deck) "A proud Aztec Man Reflects on the Cycles of Time." Like all Knights of Disks, this figure works hard to secure the future, not just for himself, but for his family. He is willing to sacrifice something in the present. This card will nurture the man by reminding him of long-range goals, and that any suffering right now will bring benefit in the future.

The Father card is the Ace of Cups, an image we think of as archetypally female – and nourishing. Genetti calls it "The Chalice of Love and the Sea of Depth." As the Father card, it tells the man he needs to learn more about emotions, how to experience them without fear or judgment.

The Child is the Queen of Wands, a concert flautist, one of many contemporary images in the deck. It indicates the power of creativity, but Genetti also stresses the way written music represents something created for the future. The card becomes the "child" of Knight of Disks work and Ace of Cups sensitivity.

The Mother, Father, Child cards come from the Wheel of Change deck, designed and drawn by Alexandra Genetti.

UNUSUAL THREE-CARD SPREADS

The following four pages deal with deeper issues than we usually find with three cards. They are also unusual in concentrating on particular parts of the deck. While we can use either one with the entire Tarot, the first works best with the Majors, and the second with the court cards, especially decks where the courts portray mythological figures.

This form illuminates some important issue in a person's life and helps the person see what spiritual "tool" he or she can use to respond to the challenge. We lay the cards out 1, 3, 2. The first card, on the left, shows the overall pattern that the person has recently experienced. The second, on the right, shows what challenges await the person. The middle card reveals what quality will help the person to meet this challenge.

The following reading was done for a woman in a painful relationship. The cards come from the Tarot of the Spirit, a Golden Dawn-based deck designed by Pamela Eakins. The cards that came up were Fool reversed, Hanged Man, and Strength. With his tame wolf at his side, the Fool leaps between worlds, from the spiritual realm of light into the dark dense world of matter. The card symbolizes all leaps we take from one state to another. Reversed, it represents the woman's state, for she described herself as forever on

For the Teacher and Helper spread, use court cards that portray mythological figures such as Mercury.

the verge of ending the relationship once and for all, yet somehow unable to do it. She has suspended herself between worlds and is in an agony of indecision. The second card shows that she needs to discover her own Strength. The figure in the picture holds the middle pillar of balance between two extremes. Caduceus snakes of healing wind around the pillar and rear above her head. The card does not show an action, but rather a state that she needs to attain so that action will become possible. The middle card, the quality that will help her meet this challenge, is the Hanged Man. The lines and geometric forces that surround the body demonstrate the Hanged Man's attachment to values and a sense of divine power in life beyond immediate crises.

The Tarot of the Spirit deck, drawn by Joyce Eakins, was used in this Spiritual Challenge reading. It teaches that action comes from surrender.

THE FOOL

0

XII

THE HANGED MAN

VIII

STRENGTH

This spread works best with court cards that show figures from myth, for example, the Mythic Tarot, Daughters of the Moon, the Elemental Tarot, Tarot of Transition, Tarot of the Orishas, the Barbara Walker Tarot. The reading here uses the Haindl Tarot.

Lay the cards out 3, 1, 2. The center card shows a role the person is acting out at this time. By comparing our behavior to a god or goddess we can get a larger view of ourselves. The card on the right shows the person's "Teacher," the one on the left his or her "Helper." The gods embody particular traits. Aphrodite, for example, signifies love. If Aphrodite becomes your teacher you will learn about desire

The creator of the Haindl Tarot deck, Hermann Haindl, drew on a specific culture for each suit.

Father of Stones in the West
King of Stones

Son of Swords in the South
Prince of Swords

Son of Cups in the North
Prince of Cups

and passion. If she appears as your helper she will lead you to love and encourage you to open your heart. The querent can take these images on any level, from psychological metaphors all the way to a statement that these beings exist in the person's life. Remember that Tarot readings are not permanent. They mirror the forces important for you right now.

The reading concerned a woman caring for a parent with a long-term illness. The cards came out as Father of Stones (Old Man), Son of Swords (Osiris), and Son of Cups (Parsifal).

Osiris showed the person's archetypal role, not just as the child, but as the care-giver. As the Egyptian god, Osiris ruled over death and rebirth. He embodies both compassion and dedication.

Another Son card forms the teacher. The Grail Knight Parsifal looks grimly at the vision in his cup, for it requires that he take responsibility for matters that are beyond his personal needs. The Grail Knight was a reluctant healer. The teacher card tells the woman to look hard at the realities of the task facing her.

"The Old Man" refers to a Native American myth of a mysterious figure who helps people in subtle ways. He makes no dramatic appearances but rather reveals his presence by his actions. The card promises the woman spiritual support in what is a difficult time.

The Page of Wands from the Mythic Tarot depicts Phrixus from the Greek myth, Jason and the Golden Fleece.

Elaine, from the Princess of Cups card, Barbara Walker Tarot.

From three cards we jump to 12! This may seem drastic, but the spread is actually a collection of single-card readings. Done at the beginning of the year (or on the person's birthday) it gives the querent guidance for each month. We lay the cards out in the form of a clock, with January at the one o'clock position, February at two, and so on through the sequence, until we reach December at 12 o'clock.

The person can indeed take each card alone, or can look for trends or rhythms in the laid-out year. Maybe the first few months will show financial problems that get worse for a while but then straighten out in late Spring. If the person does have trouble with money through March April she or he can remember the reading and its of a turn for the better in June; this may help to mind during difficult times. Or the reading may romance in one part of the year but a Hermitlike withdrawal in another.

We will look briefly through the year using this form of clock spread *(see page 307)*. See how Wands and Swords predominate. This promises to be a very active year.

It begins with the Five of Wands, which symbolizes energetic struggle. The person feels young and confident in February – Page of Wands – and this confidence grows to the Knight in March. April, however, brings a crash, for we see the Chariot reversed, followed by the painful Three of Swords in May. In June, the Four of Swords brings a period of withdrawal, followed by a consolidation of resources with the Four of Coins in July. August shows the person's confidence restored in the Six of Wands, just in time for a difficult battle in September's Five of Swords. At this point,

A spread of 12 cards laid out in the form of a clock can be used to discern trends for the coming year.

Astrology divides a chart into 12 houses.

something seems to break, for we see rejuvenation in October's Sun card, followed by two Cups cards, the Six in November, and the Seven in December. The Six carries on the theme of sharing from the Sun, while the Seven opens up the imagination to wonderful new possibilities that lie ahead.

We can use the clock form of spread in other ways, especially astrological spreads. Astrologers divide a person's chart into 12 "houses," with a theme in each house. We can use these as positions in the spread, with

Themes for the Houses

First House – outer personality, the way you look to the world.

Second House – possessions, desires, appetite.

Third House – relations other than parents, communication.

Fourth House – father, organs, home, power.

Fifth House – children, love, art.

Sixth House – health, work, surroundings.

Seventh House – marriage, partners and enemies, business.

Eighth House – death, wounds, self-sacrifice, psychic and spiritual energies.

Ninth House – travel, philosophy, vision.

Tenth House – mother, responsibility, ambition, career.

Eleventh House – friends, gossip, social involvement, ideals.

Twelfth House – unconscious forces, secrets, sorrows.

the first house at one o'clock, or compare the way the cards come out to the person's actual chart (natal or progressed).

Refer to the box *(see page 306),* for some themes for the twelve houses.

Our example uses a modern edition of the famous Tarot de Marseilles.

December

November

October

September

August

July

June

May

April

March

February

January

We come now to the most famous of all Tarot spreads — the Celtic Cross. Probably it became so prominent because Arthur Waite featured it in his book The Pictorial Key To The Tarot. Since then, most books have included a version of it. Its popularity also stems from its usefulness, for the Celtic Cross contains a mixture of predictive cards and cards that mirror the querents' desires, fears, and experiences to help them understand how they themselves shape the situation and its future.

the celtic cross

Many experienced Tarot readers, who know more spreads than they can remember, return again and again to the Celtic Cross.

Traditionally, this form of reading requires a Significator, a card drawn ahead of time to represent the person, and removed from the deck before the shuffle. Usually, this means a court card. Many people use a Page for a child, a Knight for a young adult of either gender, a Queen for a mature woman, and a King for a mature man. Some prefer not to restrict the Kings and Queens but instead separate them for their symbolic qualities. As for which suit, you can determine this through the person's character (do they seem fiery, watery, airy, or earthy?) or through the querent's Sun sign in astrology (the answer they give when someone asks, "What's your sign?"). Each sign belongs to an element, just as each element belongs to a suit. Thus, anyone born under Aries, Leo, or Sagittarius will be Wands, and so on for the other suits (see Tarot and Astrology, page 109).

There are many variations on the Celtic Cross pattern, but the following is one standard method.

When you have chosen the Significator, set it on the table and have the querent shuffle the deck. Then lay the top

An intense "magical" portrait of Arthur Edward Waite.

Choose the Significator card from the court cards.

card directly over the Significator. We call this the Cover card, and it shows the basic issue. The crossing card goes across the first horizontally. This card reveals another aspect of the situation. Together, the two form the Small Cross.

The third card, called the Root, goes below the Small Cross. The Root shows some past experience that has given rise to the current situation. Card four goes to the left of the Cover card. The Recent Past, it shows a more immediate experience that has phased out but still affects the person. Card five goes above the Small Cross, and represents the Possible Outcome, which is the overall trend or direction. Card six goes to the right of the Cover card. Called the Near Future, it shows a coming development that will affect the person but which will probably not be lasting. These six cards form the actual Celtic Cross.

The next four cards go in a row along the right side. We call them the Staff, and we lay them out from the bottom up.

Card seven signifies the Self. It shows what the person is contributing to the situation. Above that, card eight, the Environment, indicates the influence of others. Card nine reveals the querent's Hopes and Fears. The final card, the Outcome, shows the likely result of all these actions and attitudes. It does not show an inescapable fate but rather allows the person to recognize where things are headed.

Step 1

Once the Significator has been chosen, it is laid on the table. The top card, which is known as the Cover card, is laid directly over the Significator.

Step 2

The Crossing card is then laid horizontally across the first card (the Cover card). These two cards form the Small Cross.

Step 3

The third card, known as the Root, goes below the Small Cross. This card shows some experience in the past that has affected the current issue.

Step 4

Card four goes to the left of the Cover card, five goes above the Small Cross, and six goes to the right of the Cover card. This is the Celtic Cross.

Step 5

The next four cards are placed in a row at the right-hand side of the Celtic Cross. They are called the Staff, and are laid from the bottom upward.

A SAMPLE CELTIC CROSS

The following example of the Celtic Cross *(shown on page 315)* uses the Light and Shadow Tarot of Michael Goepferd. The reading concerned a woman in a long-term struggle with a family member. For Significator we chose the Queen of Pentacles.

The Cover card was the Eight of Swords reversed. The woman has felt confined and confused, but now she has begun to work her way free of some of these invisible bonds. In opposition to this, the Crossing card, the Ten of Cups, shows a vision of a harmonious family. It reflects her desire that everyone get along and restore (or create) a happy family. Below these cards we see the Four of Pentacles reversed. Right side up, this card shows a strong figure who knows how to create a psychic fortress around himself at difficult times. Reversed, however, it indicates that the woman has never learned to do this, leaving her open to attacks. In the Recent Past, however, we see the Queen of Wands, an indication of a resurgent optimism and love of life. The Possible Outcome is the Three of Cups reversed. The family may never become as open and loving as she would like. In the Near Future, the Three of Swords suggests further

The Queen of Pentacles wears stag horns, showing her connection to the beasts.

QUEEN OF PENTACLES

painful encounters to come. And yet, the card can also indicate acceptance of sorrow. The Seven of Wands reversed in the Self position says that she wants to stop struggling. She does not want to have to defend herself, deal with crises, act like a warrior.

In a reading that is about conflict, the Environment card becomes important, for it shows how some quality of the other person affects the querent. Here we see the Tower card reversed. The family member is facing some crisis of her own. She fears that her whole world will crumble and leave her naked and destroyed. The reversal of the card stresses her attempt to head this off. In such a state she cannot help but lash out at anyone nearby.

The Hopes and Fears card is the Ace of Pentacles reversed. The querent fears that nothing positive can grow out of this situation. Right side up, the figures all cradle against the Pentacle. Reversed, the family offers no shelter.

The Outcome card returns her to the liberation theme of the first. The High Priestess shows her both aware and detached. She will learn how to separate from the anxieties of the people around her, and her own disappointed longing for

In its position as the Crossing card, the Ten of Cups shows the querent's desire for a harmonious family life.

Details from the Light and Shadow Tarot of Michael Goepferd.

the perfect family. This detachment may allow her to express what Brian Williams, commentator for this deck, calls the High Priestess' "loving, forgiving moral conscience."

The High Priestess is
the Outcome card.

The Three of Cups
reversed is the
Possible Outcome
card.

The Three of Swords
is the Near Future
card.

The Ace of Pentacles
reversed is the
Hopes and Fears
card.

The Ten of Cups is
the Crossing Card.

The Queen of Wands
is the Recent Past
card.

The Eight of Swords
reversed is the
Cover card.

The Tower reversed
is the Environment
card.

The Four of
Pentacles reversed
is the Root card.

The Seven of Wands
reversed is the Self
card.

Many spreads exist to explore relationship questions, all the way from "Does he love me?" to "How do I get out of this?" The following one is unique in that it treats the relationship itself as a kind of third person, with its own needs and desires.

a relationship spread

The idea for this approach came from all those cards in the Waite deck where we see one figure presiding over two others. They begin with the Hierophant, the Lovers, and the Chariot and carry through to the Minor Arcana, with such cards as the Six of Pentacles. In all of these we might describe the two on the sides as the couple, and the character in the middle as the relationship they have created.

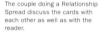

The couple doing a Relationship Spread discuss the cards with each other as well as with the reader.

The reading works well when two people come together. They can mix the cards with four hands and then the reader can lay them out as a grid, with each question receiving three answers. The particular questions used draw from the work of Gail Fairfield, in her book *Choice Centered Tarot*.

In the first row, the husband fulfills his responsibility to his family but remains distant. The people in the picture do not speak and they carry sorrow with them. The wife takes on all the emotional burdens of the relationship. The relationship

itself hangs on tightly to what will keep it together, the history, the rituals, and the shared economics.

The next line, Wants, shows the couple's fantasies. The man wants magic and excitement. The woman wants a cozy joyous family. The relationship, however, wants not to be a Devil, oppressive and imprisoning. Remember that in the Waite deck the Devil is a kind of distortion of the Lovers. The Really Wants line shows more modest desires. The husband wants not to have to work at it. For too long the marriage has seemed like work to him. The wife really wants a declaration of love, possibly a renewed commitment. The relationship wants only to keep back the problems.

When we look at Needs, we see some dramatic changes. The husband needs a different kind of magic than he imagines. He needs a secure and joyous environment, in which he can feel that love comes as a gift, not a requirement. The woman needs to take charge more. And the relationship needs hope, and emotions poured out openly.

How do they satisfy those needs? The husband should take action, possibly declare his needs – and his love – more openly. The Eight of Wands sometimes bears the title, "The Arrows of Love." The wife can lead the two of them out of their grayness and into a celebration. If she lets herself become the King of Wands (her Need) she can initiate the love she seeks as the Page. And the relationship can satisfy its needs by a surrender to trust.

	HUSBAND	WIFE	RELATIONSHIP

1
How do you behave?

2
What do you want?

3
What do you really want?

4
What do you need?

5
How do you satisfy those needs?

Many people want the Tarot to illuminate their path in life, how they can fulfill themselves. While the cards rarely can give precise directions ("Move to Colorado and open a rare books store") they can give a sense of what we need.

the sacred quest spread

This spread bases itself on the structure of myths and fairy tales, in which the hero must fulfill a quest. The cards are laid out in a six-pointed star, with a final card in the center.

The reading *(shown on page 323)* concerned a woman unhappy with her work. We used the Arthurian Tarot (also called "Hallowquest"), designed by Caitlín and John Matthews, and painted by Miranda Gray. The cards came out as 1. Stone King, 2. Grail King, 3. Spear Hallow (Ace of Wands), 4. Guinevere (Empress) reversed, 5. Prydwen (Chariot), 6. Sword Maiden, 7. Sword Knight.

Right away we see the archetypal quality of the reading. Four of the seven are court cards, mythic personalities. Two more are Major Arcana, and the seventh, Spear Hallow, is an Ace.

The quest is to become the King of Stones. This figure represents power and responsibility, the guardian and protector of knowledge. The path is another King, of the Grail itself. This reinforces the idea of seeking knowledge, for the Matthews describe the character as "Guardian of the hidden mysteries." These two cards suggest a path of

Knights prayed for guidance before beginning a quest. Tarot readers might feel the same way.

great power, possibly dealing with esoteric ideas. The path leads her to the Spear Hallow (Ace of Wands). This is a card of healing through the beginning of projects. Her need to embody the two Kings leads her to begin something important in her life, perhaps the study of spiritual teachings.

Guinevere (Empress) reversed opposes her. This implies a lack of faith in her own power and passion. What aids her is Prydwen (Chariot), a card of confidence, discipline, and courage. She will meet obstacles (the storm-tossed boat) but she can journey through them.

The myth of Camelot inspired the Arthurian Tarot.

For sacrifice we find another character, the Sword Maiden (Page of Swords). This figure emphasizes the idea of sacrifice itself, for the text tells us "she cuts through difficulties by taking the way of self-sacrifice." The woman may have to give up ordinary plans and goals to achieve her higher destiny.

When she does this, she becomes the Sword Knight, a heroic figure, fearless and brilliant intellectually, "the upholder of the Sword of Light."

4. What opposes you?

2. What path are you on?

1. What is your quest?

7. What will you become?

6. What must you sacrifice?

The mythic pictures of the Arthurian Tarot help delineate the idea of the quest.

5. What aids you?

3. Where does it lead you?

This fascinating spread comes from a Tarot reader in Denmark, Anita Jensen. It uses the querent's body as the basis to explore complex attitudes and behaviors. With someone very open you can ask the querent to lie down on the floor (or a massage table) and place the cards directly on the body, then remove them and put them alongside so the person can sit up and look at the pattern they form.

the body spread

The first card goes on the forehead and describes what the person is thinking. The second goes over the mouth and shows what the person is saying. Notice the possibility for contradictions between these two. The third card goes over the heart (or in the center of the chest at the heart level) and tells what the person feels about the issue. The fourth card goes on the solar plexus (the gut) and shows what the person knows deep down. The fifth card goes over the groin area and says what the person desires (not necessarily sexual desire).

Lying down with the Tarot cards on your body can be a playful or intense experience.

For the final four cards you need to determine the person's "major" and "minor" hands. For right-handed people the right hand is major and the left minor. For left-handed people the opposite is true. Card six goes on the minor hand and represents what the person holds back. Card seven goes on the major hand and signifies what the person gives to others. Card eight goes on the minor foot and shows past experience – where the person is coming from. Card nine goes on the major foot and indicates where the person is headed.

Our sample reading concerned a man who found his partner overpowering. He wanted a way to find and express his own strength. Temperance reversed at the forehead describes his agitated state. He cannot stay calm, and would lie awake at night, angry at his girlfriend's behavior and his own weakness. At the mouth, the Hermit shows his declaring a need to be separate. He cannot express his disturbance except to say that he wants solitude.

At the heart, we find the Speaker of Rivers (King of Cups) reversed. The Speaker cards share their mastery of the suit elements with others. Rivers is the suit of emotion and love, very fitting for the heart position. But we find it reversed here, showing that he does not communicate – does not speak – what he feels. What he knows – the solar plexus – is Justice. Deep down, he knows that he cannot accept an unjust unequal relationship. Perhaps the card also signifies some truth about himself that he does not want to face. At the groin, the Sun shows a desire for a simple happy relationship, a desire at odds with his thoughts and feelings and beliefs, and even his statements.

He holds back the Five of Birds (Five of Swords), the belief that he can free himself only through the destruction of the current situation. He gives out the Five of Rivers (Five of Cups) reversed, uncertain whether the relationship is already lost. The minor foot shows the Lovers reversed. He comes from a sense of the relationship as unloving and already in the past. We see him stepping toward the Six of Trees, an image of confidence as a man walks without fear through a frightening landscape.

Right
For this reading, we used the Shining Woman Tarot, designed and drawn by myself.

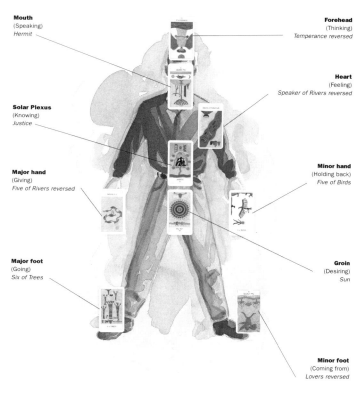

Mouth
(Speaking)
Hermit

Forehead
(Thinking)
Temperance reversed

Heart
(Feeling)
Speaker of Rivers reversed

Solar Plexus
(Knowing)
Justice

Major hand
(Giving)
Five of Rivers reversed

Minor hand
(Holding back)
Five of Birds

Major foot
(Going)
Six of Trees

Groin
(Desiring)
Sun

Minor foot
(Coming from)
Lovers reversed

Spreads exist to tackle many difficult subjects. As you get used to the way they work, you may want to design spreads on the spot for people's individual questions. Clearly this involves discussion with the querent. It cannot work for readers who do not want to know the issue ahead of time. It also does not work for querents without any special concern, who just want to see what the cards will show them.

your own tarot spread

This spread is for people who need to address a particular problem. Doing a spread specific to them can ensure all their questions are covered.

It is important for the reader to find out what the querent really wants to achieve from a Tarot reading.

Start by asking what the person wants to know. It might help you to write down the points they raise as they speak. Most people will say only one or two broad sentences, so that the next phase requires you to open up the question. For instance, someone might say, "I want to know why I keep doing the same thing over and over." The first position would look at the recurring pattern. You would ask him to describe what happens. He might answer, "I start projects with great enthusiasm and then suddenly it all falls apart. I've changed jobs five times, I fall madly in love and then get bored with the person." One position in the spread could represent "What happens at the beginning of new experiences," and another "What ends them." A third card could symbolize the "bridge" between the beginning and end.

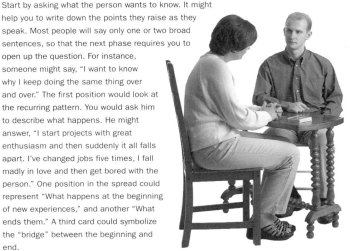

You might ask the person to describe more clearly what occurs. Do his projects fail? Or does he become scared? He might answer, "No, nothing terrible happens. I just get bored. I lose all my energy. Finally I feel panicky and I have to get out." You would plan a card for the boredom and another for the panic. If he says, "I was like this as a child too," you could include a card for "childhood history."

You could then add some questions generally good for people with problem issues. "What lies underneath this pattern?" And "What does she need to learn?" Others could include "What blocks him from changing it?", "What will help him break this pattern?", and "What can he do right now?"

You can do a similar process with many other questions, from small issues to fundamental problems. If someone wanted help choosing where to go on a vacation you could have them describe the various options with the attractions and potential problems for each place, and then draw a card for all the

The meaning of the Star, from the Ukiyoë Tarot, would depend greatly on the specific question in the reading.

XVII   拾七

THE STAR

星

different points. If a man wanted to look at his relationship with his children, you could discuss the particular questions he has about his own behavior, past actions, and so on, and draw a card for each one plus cards for his special connections to each child, what approach will help him with them as a group, what actions will work best with each child individually, and so on.

Once you begin this process you may discover that you prefer your own Tarot spread to fixed spreads for your readings.

Consider each of the various positions of the reading. How would the meanings of these two cards differ from place to place?

Designing a structure

Now that the two of you have worked out the questions, you may want to design a structure. If there are levels of meaning you could do it in rows. Or you could ask the querent if he prefers, say, a star or a circle. Here are the questions for the man who quits everything.

1. Recurring pattern.
2. What lies underneath.
3. What he needs to learn.
4. Enthusiasm at start.
5. What happens at the end.
6. What happens in the middle.
7. Boredom.
8. Panic.
9. Influence of childhood experience.
10. What will break the pattern.
11. What blocks him.
12. What will overcome the block.
13. What he can do right now.

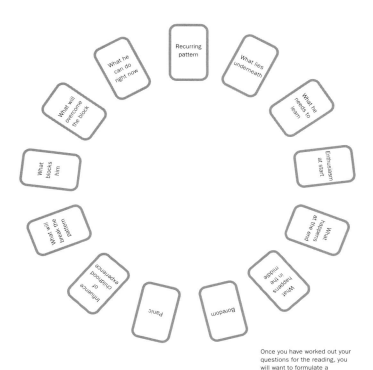

Once you have worked out your questions for the reading, you will want to formulate a structure. A circle is a common design.

The idea of designing your own spread comes from the work of Gail Fairfield. The same author has suggested a way to use Tarot cards to interpret dreams.

dream work

Dreams confuse and tantalize us. What do they mean? What do their images symbolize? We ask these same questions about Tarot cards. Unlike dreams, however, Tarot cards come complete with a system of explanations. And if we apply the cards to our dreams we may gain a greater understanding of them.

The basic technique is simple. Write down the dream. When you have the dream on paper, go back and separate it into sections. If something special happened before you went to sleep, or you react strongly when you wake up, include these as well.

Write down your dreams as soon you wake.

The distorted images of many of our dreams – a moon grown too big for the sky, say, or memories of places that are familiar but changed, can be hard to interpret. The Tarot can help you to unravel them.

The dream

Consider this dream, reported by a musician.

"I dream I find myself in front of the house where I grew up. Everything looks covered in mud. I go inside. Sheets cover everything. There are holes in the sheets and I can see my toys underneath. I smell food and rush into the kitchen, thinking I will see my grandmother. Instead, I'm in my bedroom. A grand piano has replaced my bed. I pick up the music scattered on it and study it carefully. I wake up anxious."

Now that she has seen some of the dream's hidden messages she can work with the dream and the reading further *(the reading is shown on pages 338–9)*. She might meditate on a particular card, such as the Hierophant, to see what Chiron conceals in his cave, or the Eight of Cups to follow Psyche into the "Underworld" of her childhood. Or she might draw or write a new version of the dream and change it by including some of the characters and insights from the cards.

1. She finds herself in front of her old home.
2. The house is covered in mud.
3. She goes inside.
4. Sheets cover everything.
5. She can see toys through the holes.
6. She smells food, looks for her grandmother.
7. She goes to her bedroom.
8. A grand piano has replaced her bed.
9. She studies the pages of music.
10. Anxiety waking up.

If you dreamed of a grand piano what might it mean to you? If you dreamed of a toy, it may evoke specific childhood events. The cards can help trigger such memories.

1. Two of Wands. The hero Jason stands at the dark cave of his teacher, the centaur Chiron. He has just learned of his royal heritage, hidden from him. The house – the dream – contains some truth the woman does not recognize.

2. Ace of Wands. Zeus, king of the gods. He wears the golden fleece Jason must seek. This too shows the "treasure" inside the abandoned home.

3. Ace of Swords. Athena, goddess of justice. By entering the house Athena I actively seeking the truth.

4. Ace of Pentacles. The god Poseidon. The card signifies wealth and achievement. The sheets conceal her power.

5. Hierophant. Chiron, seen again through the "hole" of the cave. The toys are not trivial but represent what she has learned from her life.

6. Six of Wands. Jason's triumph. Food and her grandmother signify getting what she wants in life.

EIGHT OF CUPS

7. Eight of Cups. The heroine Psyche travels to the Underworld to meet Persephone, goddess of death and rebirth. She cannot get the "food" she desires until she has "descended" to childhood memories for renewal.

TEN OF PENTACLES

8. Ten of Pentacles reversed. A happy family scene. Reversed, the card shows that the piano – her musical studies – will not satisfy her need to reconnect to her past.

FOUR OF WANDS

9. Four of Wands. Jason and his companions prepare to set forth on their quest. Her study of the paper shows that she is ready to make a quest for self-knowledge and an understanding of her history.

10. The Moon. Hecate, goddess of the Underworld. Her anxiety tells her she has not finished with this dream and its "treasure."

The deck used was the Mythic Tarot, based on Greek mythology. Tricia Newell drew the images under the direction of Juliet Sharman-Burke and Liz Greene.

things to do with tarots

In the Renaissance, people knew the Tarot as a game. Over time readings became the primary use of the cards, so that most people think the mysterious inventors of the Tarot designed it just for that. But there are many other ways in which we can use the cards to explore their wisdom. Aside from readings, how do we tap their complex truths? In this part of the book, we learn how we can use the cards in creative projects — in music and storytelling, for instance. Share the experience of the cards with your friends by playing charades, rummy, or other games. Exercise with the cards or imitate the bodily posture of the characters. Create your own deck with images that have particular relevance for you. Meditate with the Tarot and explore the cards in depth. Use the cards to train and exercise your will. There are numerous ways to help us to get to know our cards better. And once we have done the reading, and absorbed the information and lessons, we can use the cards to make the changes in ourselves and our lives that the reading itself recommends.

Whether you are new to the world of Tarot entirely or have just acquired a wonderful new deck of cards, you will want to get to know your cards that bit better. We can usually do this through the careful study of their symbols, the memorization of their meanings, and with practical work in readings (with one eye on the book, of course). However, we can use the cards in more creative ways too, to learn what messages they can release to us. You could put together a few friends to play some of the games mentioned below, or to act out a few cards. A sense of humor will help here. You can have a great time and still learn about the cards.

unusual ways to get to know your cards

Something that will help you remember the Major Arcana cards is to use them in physical exercise. If you do aerobics or anything else that involves counting, substitute the cards for numbers. As you stretch, or go up and down steps, say to yourself, "Fool, Magician, High Priestess, Empress …" See if you can flash the card or its basic quality in your mind as you say its name.

A more direct way to use the body involves postures. Try to find a posture that evokes the card. You can imitate the character in the picture. For the Magician, stand with one arm up (holding a wand of some kind), and the other pointed down. For the World, stand with one leg behind the other, and arms out. If you're agile you could do the Hanged Man by standing on your head, yoga-style (you'll find this a lot easier, and safer, against a wall). Other cards, such as the High Priestess or the Chariot, might require a little more invention to find a posture that truly brings out their quality.

The paintings of poet and mystic William Blake inspired the William Blake Tarot.

One way to get to know a deck in greater depth is to ask it questions about itself. Mix the cards and turn them over as if for a reading, but instead of the usual questions speak directly to the cards. For example –"What special message

do you bring?" "What do you want to teach me?" "What do I need to work with you?"

Michele Jackson, the creator of a major Tarot Website on the Internet, reported that the first question she always asks of a new deck is, "How will we get along?"

Let's look at some of these questions with a specific deck – the William Blake Tarot. This deck was created by Ed Buryn from the art and poetry of the 18th century English mystic, William Blake. I chose the following three questions:

What do you want to teach me? Four of Poetry (Four of Wands), "Harmony." The picture shows a man and woman looking up at a heavenly light. The text in the picture describes how love and harmony "around our souls intwine."

The deck seeks to teach this marvelous lesson.

What do you ask of me? Two of Poetry, "Individuality." "Every Man's Wisdom is peculiar to his own Individuality."

This deck expects me to confront the cards myself rather than depend on the book, or previous studies of other Tarot decks, or, maybe especially, scholarly studies of the works of William Blake.

What relationship can we have? Four of Music (Four of Cups), "Musing." The picture indicates a joyous relationship. Old men perform music while children play by a tree. The old men might represent William Blake himself, while the child could symbolize myself or anyone who looks at the deck with Individuality. The subtitle, "Musing," also hints that this deck, so devoted to creativity, could act as a muse to my own work.

Left
Some decks seem especially eager to share their wisdom and point of view.

Numbers and daily life

We mentioned that some people choose a card a day with a new deck. They then watch how that day's events reflect the card. You can look for other things as well. Notice how often the card's number comes up.

For example, if the card was the World, you might watch for the number 24 on license plates, room numbers, chapter headings, dates, television, and so on. Or you might notice if the card comes up in some way in other people's behavior, or overheard bits of conversation. "I think the world of you," someone might say to a friend, or a relative might tell you of a success in business or some other great moment.

You can do things that will reinforce the theme of the card. Go dancing for the World, do something impulsive for the Fool, assess your finances for the Four of Pentacles. The more imaginative your approach, the more likely the card will stay in your mind.

Standing in the Magician posture opens the body to a flow of energy.

For many historians, the Tarot began as a game called *Tarocchi,* or in French, *Les Tarots.* People still play this game, the ancestor of bridge. You even can play it symbolically, that is, follow the game according to its rules, but look at the various interactions and the end result as a kind of Tarot reading. A number of people have developed games more directly connected to the cards' symbolic messages. Some of these, for example Tarot charades, help us to get to know the cards in a more lively way. Others, such as Tarot Rummy, give us information about ourselves.

tarot games

In Tarot charades one person from each team chooses a card at random. The person must act out the card in such a way that the person's teammates can guess which card it is. The person can choose one of two ways to perform the card. He or she can mime the picture literally, or else behave according to the card's quality. The first approach requires silence, the second allows speech. For example, suppose a woman draws the Waite Ten of Wands. She may walk slowly, bowed down, and with her hands up as if she is carrying ten long sticks. Or, she may choose the second method and look weary while saying something like, "Oh, what a burdensome life I have. Everything always depends on me. I just wish I could put my burdens down for a while."

One variation on Tarot charades, developed by Danish Tarotist Helle Agathe Beierholm, allows two people to play together. Each chooses a card without showing it to the other. Then they must stay in character while playing off against each other. Say the first person chooses the Waite Seven of Cups, the card of fantasies. The other chooses the Five of Pentacles, the card of the two ragged people limping along in the snow. The first begins, "What shall we do today? Maybe we'll win the lottery. Rich beyond our wildest dreams! Or maybe we can study Kabbalah. Let's learn the entire Kabbalah today!"

Early Tarot decks were used to play *Tarocchi*.

The other can say, "Oh, I feel so weak, so helpless. I know you'll stay with me, no matter how wretched we become. I just hope we can survive." The first replies, "Are you sick? Maybe you only have two weeks to live. Let's take a trip

Other Tarot games

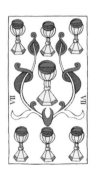

tarot rummy

This interesting game (I learned it from Mary Greer) produces a kind of interactive reading. Any number above two can play but it works best with four people. Someone mixes the deck and deals out four cards to each player. Everyone then gives one card to the person on the left. They then give one card to the person two seats away. Finally they give one card to the person on the right. Each person ends up with four cards, one from each player, and one they kept for themselves. They then show their cards and describe what meanings they see in them. They also might say what prompted them to give the specific cards to each person, and why they kept the one they held.

around the world." They continue this for a set time limit (two minutes works well), and then they have to guess each other's cards.

Mary Greer developed this game as what she calls "an icebreaker version of Rummy." Greer uses several decks for this one, so that it becomes a way for people in a class or study group, who all use different decks, to learn about each other's Tarots. All the decks go into a "pond" and then each person fishes out two cards. They keep one and give the other to the person on the left. Each person then describes what they see in the card they kept, the one they gave away, and the one they received.

Another game involves group storytelling. Everyone sits in the circle with a deck in the center. The first person takes a card and begins a story based on the picture. When he or she has reached an exciting moment, the next person takes a card and must continue the story from this new picture (see also Tarot, Music and Storytelling, page 361).

For further ways to play with the cards, look through the book *Tarot Games* by Maura Shaw and Cait Johnson.

Seven of cups, Tarot de Marseilles (far left) and Ten of Wands, Morgan Greer Tarot. Tarot games can be played with any deck of your choice.

We have said that Tarot differs from astrology by having no lifetime symbol, such as the Sun sign from a person's birth chart. Many people, however, find it valuable to discover a symbolic image that will in fact give them a way to look at their recurrent patterns and life challenges.

personality, soul, and year cards

The following method allows you to find cards that reveal your "personality" and "soul." You also can use it to discover a card for the current year.

The system comes from teacher and writer Angeles Arrien, in her book *The Tarot Handbook*. Mary K. Greer has developed it further in her *Tarot Constellations*.

Write down your birth date in numbers. Do it in three lines (*see the box on page 352 for examples*). Add these numbers until you get a single number. Now add the digits in that number. This is called "reduction." If the number reduces to a double digit number 22 or below, that number reveals the personality card. In our first example, 20 is the number of the Tarot card Judgement. You can then find the soul number by adding the two digits of the personality number. With 20, 2+0=2, the High Priestess. If the numbers add up to a single digit, this new number forms both the personality and the soul number. Our second example reduced to 9, the Hermit. The Hermit functions as both the personality and soul card.

If the number reduces to a double digit number above 22, reduce it once more. In our third example, 25 is a number above 22, so that we add 2+5 and get 7, the number of the

How to find your cards

Write down your birth date in numbers. Do it in three lines. Here are three examples:

Jan. 22, 1950	June 18, 1983	May 17, 1974
1	6	5
22	18	17
1950	1983	1974

Add these numbers until you get a single number.

1	6	5
22	18	17
<u>1950</u>	<u>1983</u>	<u>1974</u>
1973	2007	1996

Now add the digits in that number. This is called "reduction."

$$1+9+7+3=20 \qquad 2+0+0+7=9 \qquad 1+9+9+6=25$$

You can find your personality card by reducing your birth date down to a number below 22.

Chariot. In this case, therefore, the Chariot becomes both the personality and the soul card. According to Arrien, the personality card shows "your expression in the outer world, your talent, gifts, resources; and how others see you." The soul card reveals "the deepest core of who you are."

One number reduces twice. 19 gives us 1+9=10, but 10 then gives 1+0=1. In this case, Arrien describes 19 (the Sun) as the personality card, 1 (the Magician) as the soul card, with 10 (the Wheel of Fortune) as a symbol of creativity.

This system produces some interesting combinations. 17 and 8, the Star and Strength, go together harmoniously. But what of 16 and 7, the Tower and the Chariot? Or 15 and 6, the Devil and the Lovers? Do these pairs show a sharp contrast between what people show to the world and their deep selves? 22 and 4 are a special pair. For the purpose of this system, 22 represents the 22nd card, the unnumbered Fool. The Fool shows us a personality that is free, spontaneous, and instinctive, the very image of the eternal child. But 2+2=4, the Emperor, the symbol of maturity, responsibility, rationality, and control. The two cards suggest a person who displays a childlike persona to others but underneath hides a more mature sense of his or her place and power in the world.

For dates that reduce to a single number for both personality and soul, we can think of an implied higher number. For example, June 18, 1983 reduced directly to 9, the Hermit. 9 implies 18, the Moon, for 1+8=9. In these

XIX — THE SUN

I — THE MAGICIAN

X — WHEEL OF FORTUNE

The number 19 reduces twice, first to 10, and then to one. This gives us three cards – the Sun, the Magician, and the Wheel of Fortune.

cases we might think of the "invisible" higher number as a symbol of the person's challenges in life. Mary Greer calls it the "hidden factor" and describes it as qualities that act as a teacher.

The four lowest numbers, 1–4, all have two possible higher numbers. 19 and 10 for 1, 20 and 11 for 2, 21 and 12 for 3, and 22 and 13 for 4. If the person gets one of these higher numbers the other one can represent the challenge. For example, 21 would mean the World for the personality card, the Empress for the soul card, and the Hanged Man for the challenge. These alternative higher numbers are also hidden factor or shadow cards.

Sun signs

If you know astrology, and the astrological correlations of the Major Arcana, you might want to see if your personality and soul cards correspond to your chart in any special way. My own soul card is Strength, and my Sun sign is Leo. These two reinforce each other. However, if someone with a soul card of Strength was born under Pisces, the combination might produce more complex issues of Fire and Water.

You also can use this numerological technique to determine a card for the year. Do the same process but instead of your birth year write in the current year. In the year 2000, the person born on January 22, 1950 would write down

You can also use numerological reduction to determine a card for the year.

$$
\begin{array}{r}
1 \\
22 \\
\underline{2000} \\
2023 = 7 \text{ the Chariot}
\end{array}
$$

Beginning on January 22, 2000 the person will embark on a Chariot year, to face issues of will and mastery. The following year, 2001, the theme will change to 8, Strength.

We think of the Tarot as a colorful set of symbols. Before the meanings, however, came the images. Even if someone designs the Tarot cards according to a fixed set of ideas and symbols, we still look at the picture before we read the text. And these pictures have a way of inspiring us beyond the original intent.

making your own deck

38

Many people who never read with the cards, and have no interest in Kabbalah or other systems, are still devoted to Tarot as a beautiful art form.

Stuart Kaplan, author of the *Tarot Encyclopedia*, not only has published most of the contemporary Tarot decks, including decks he himself has commissioned in different styles, such as the Japanese Ukiyoë deck, but he has also built up one of the largest and most comprehensive collections of original Tarot art in the world.

Robert O'Neill, author of *Tarot Symbolism,* and someone who sees the Major Arcana as a kind of mystical road map, has never done a reading in his many years long love affair with the Tarot. He does, however, use the cards in a very special way. He creates decks. Not one deck, but many. His decks are all formed from carefully staged photographs, complete with costumes, dramatic lighting, and stunning special effects.

The Queen of Wands and King of Cups from the Ukiyoë Tarot, which was commissioned by Stuart Kaplan.

Creating a Deck
Should you create your own deck? If you believe that the truth of the Tarot lies in a set of symbols fixed for all time, then the answer is probably no. And yet, the Golden Dawn

The BOTA Tarot deck is designed so that you color in the pictures yourself.

taught that very idea, and all of its members did indeed create their own cards. They copied Mathers' original, or they copied copies of the copies. If you have decided firmly on your deck, you might want to copy it and make it your own. The art may end up cruder (or possibly improved) but you will have a unique Tarot. Or you might try the BOTA approach and color your favorite deck. You can do that in two ways. Copy the original in black and white and then color it, or else paint right onto the cards themselves.

A number of people have published recolored versions of the Rider-Waite cards. Frankie Albano did a brighter version, while Mary Hanson-Roberts did a softer, more pastel version in her Universal Rider. Carol Herzer, who has created many decks, including abstract designs, did a radical psychedelic version in her Illuminated Rider.

If you copy a deck or color or paint one, you may wish to change it. You could add small symbols of your own, pictures of animals, or key words. You also might want to take something out. A number of people, who like the art in the Harris-Crowley Thoth cards, but do not like the theme titles, have simply left them out of the margins.

You may find you want to create an entirely new deck. You could choose a theme. For instance, if you have always loved fairy tales you might want to create a deck of illustrations from your favorite stories. Or you might want to use your own cultural background, or even family history.

You can buy card stock at art supply stores. Stock comes in large sheets, in different colors and thicknesses. The store will be able to cut the sheets into cards for you.

If you believe you cannot draw (remember that all children draw naturally) you can create your cards through photographs or collage. For photos you could set out symbolic objects or stage your friends in the costumes and action you want for your pictures. Jennifer Moore created her deck, The Healing Tarot, over several years of carefully staged photographs.

Draw your own deck but add personal symbols.

Both Robert O'Neill and Jennifer Moore are masters of photographic technique, but you do not need to study special effects for years to create a deck this way. Imagination and a spirit of play will carry you very far.

You can paint your own copy of an original card.

To create a collage deck, assemble images you like from books or magazines. You might even add small objects, such as marked stones, or an old key, or a pressed flower. For your finished deck, you can use the actual assembled pieces of art, or you can photograph them to create a set of uniform cards. Photographs also will work well for making copies of hand-painted decks, either to give to your friends or for your own daily use.

If you wish to make your own deck, give yourself time and the freedom to experiment. Think of it as a way to trust your own instincts and acquired wisdom.

Create a collage deck with cutouts and other small objects.

We can use Tarot cards in creative ways beyond the art of making our own deck. One interesting method involves music. Paul Foster Case, the founder of the Builders of the Adytum (BOTA), lists a musical tone for each Major Arcana card. We can derive themes for songs or classical compositions by shuffling the cards and choosing a preset number. Or you might see which Major Arcana cards come up in a reading and use them for a song. Similarly, you could take your favorite musical themes and discover what Major Arcana cards hide within them. Opposite are Case's attributions:

Case did not attribute a musical tone to the Sun or the Hermit.

Nine of
Cups

Knight of
Swords

Six of
Swords

Eight of
Cups

Storytelling

We also can use the Tarot in storytelling. The great Italian writer Italo Calvino called the Tarot "a machine for telling stories." The phrase comes in the afterword to his novel *The Castle of Crossed Destinies*. In this clever story a group of strangers find themselves stranded in a castle where a curse prevents them from speaking. They find, however, a set of Visconti-Sforza Tarot cards, and one by one they turn over cards to show their companions. With each person, the narrator interprets the cards to form a tale. Here is a brief excerpt: "Do you want riches (Coins) or power (Swords) or wisdom (Cups)? Choose at once."

It was a stern and radiant archangel (Knight of Swords) who addressed this question to him, and our hero answered quickly, crying out: "I choose riches (Coins)!"

"You shall have Clubs!" was the reply of the mounted archangel, as city and tree dissolved into smoke and the thief hurtled down through crashing, broken branches into the midst of the forest.

Calvino may have deliberately chosen cards to construct the stories he wanted to tell. Other people, including myself, have used the Tarot to improvise entirely new stories. The method involves shuffling the cards, and choosing several at random. Rather than interpret these as a personal reading, the storyteller will look at the pictures to see what characters or plot they might suggest. If you want to try this, you should do your best to let go of the cards' traditional or "official" meanings, and instead let your imagination roam freely over the possible stories.

For example, several years ago I developed a story with the Waite deck. The first card was the Nine of Cups. Out of this card came the idea of a stealer of souls, an immortal magician who plucks the souls from the victims whom he invites to grand balls at his palace, and who now move through the world empty of emotion or desire. A later card, the Knight of Cups, inspired the character of Dream Walker, who struggles with his enemy entirely within the dreams of the imprisoned souls. The other characters helped to fill in the supporting characters and the plot.

Some decks work better than others for this process. Choose decks such as the Waite-Smith, with vivid action scenes on each card. When you draw the cards, let your imagination run free. Give the pictures a chance to take you somewhere unexpected.

Calvino used the Tarot to outline a series of tales. Other writers have used the cards as themes in their work. In Marsha Norman's *The Fortune Teller* the heroine uses Tarot to uncover truths she may not want to know. Charles Williams' classic *The Greater Trumps* explores the Tarot's mystical possibilities through a supernatural thriller. One very unusual novel, Tim Powers' *Last Call,* mixes Tarot, poker, and the myth of the Holy Grail to create an amazing mystery adventure set in Las Vegas.

Five of Wands

Eight of Coins

Nine of Cups

King of Cups

THE INTERPRETATION OF TALES

The Tarot can combine with storytelling in another unusual way. Instead of using the cards to create original stories, we can also use them to interpret more traditional ones.

This approach treats a tale or myth in the same way in which we look at dreams. That is, we separate the story in its parts, mix the cards, and draw one card for each part. The pictures and symbols on the cards illuminate our understanding of the tale.

Here is a very short but famous Jewish legend which I interpreted using The Shining Woman deck of cards. The story concerns four famous rabbis from 2,000 years ago who studied and meditated until they were able to enter Paradise and see God. Despite its brevity, the story has fostered many volumes of interpretation, including at least two modern novels. This version comes from Howard Schwartz, in his anthology *Gabriel's Palace: Jewish Mystical Tales:*

Rabbinical commentaries return again and again to important stories.

> *Four sages entered Paradise –*
> *Ben Azzai, Ben Zoma, Aher, and Rabbi Akiba. Ben Azzai looked and died.*
> *Ben Zoma looked and lost his mind.*
> *Aher cut himself off from his fathers and died.*
> *Only Rabbi Akiba entered and departed in peace.*

To interpret this legend I asked the cards six questions –
"What is Paradise?" and "How do we enter it?" plus one
separate card for each of the four rabbis.

What is Paradise? Nine of Birds. This card plunges us into
a paradox. Instead of an image of pleasure, or immortality,
we see a tomb. A goddess figure emerges from the rocks,
with an owl on top of them. The goddess signifies rebirth,
so that the tomb becomes a passage to transformation.
The owl represents mystery. Thus, Paradise becomes a
place of mystery and darkness, where everything we
thought we knew breaks down and becomes transformed.

The owl that appears on the Nine
of Birds card represents piercing
the veil of mystery.

How do we enter there? Temperance. We need to keep
our balance even as we rise to the level of the angels.
Temperance comes after Death, at the end of the second
level of the Major Arcana. We go through various stages
of knowledge and initiation until at
Temperance we are ready for the great work of
the final row of trumps, ready, in other words, to
enter Paradise.

Following the two general questions, I
asked one question specifically for each
of the four rabbis.

Ben Azzai – Nine of Rivers. One of two "Jewish"
cards in the deck, this picture derives from a 16th century
Kabbalist creation myth. According to Rabbi Isaac Luria,

This Indian miniature shows two female ascetics charming snakes – the symbol of kundalini energy.

when God created the world He sent His light into vessels. The lower vessels, however, could not contain such power. They shattered so that we live in a broken universe. Ben Azzai was such a vessel. His devotion brought him to an experience he could not contain. It overwhelmed him utterly and he died as a result.

Ben Zoma – Speaker of Trees (King of Wands). Trees is the suit of Fire, the element of ecstatic experience. We see a snake rising up a Tree of Life to a face that glows with golden light and a violet halo. In yoga, the snake symbolizes kundalini energy. We experience "Paradise" when this energy uncoils up the spine to burst out of the violet-colored "crown chakra." Yogic practice warns us that to do so without proper grounding – without Temperance – can result in madness. This is what happened to the rabbi Ben Zoma.

Aher – Ace of birds. Here we see an owl staring intently. Aher was said to have seen the angel Metatron seated on a throne alongside God. He thought this meant Heaven contained two powers, not one. Since Jews believe above all else in One God, Aher lost his faith and became an enemy of his people. In the Ace of Birds we see him looking deeply into the mystery, but without the Temperance of true understanding.

Akiba – Four of Rivers. This is the other Jewish-inspired card. We see a man in a Hebrew prayer shawl. Above him a ram's horn (blown on the Jewish New Year) sends out golden light. A dove flies in the light. A ragged robe, symbol of the man's old way of life, floats off downstream. This ability to accept transformation allows Rabbi Akiba to enter and depart in peace.

The Shining Woman deck draws on sacred traditions going back 50,000 years.

9 of BIRDS

TEMPERANCE
14

9 of RIVERS

SPEAKER of TREES

ACE of BIRDS

4 of RIVERS

Just as we can use the Tarot to interpret dreams and myths, so we can ask it questions about life. The Tarot works so well in readings because it is a book of wisdom. We can draw on that wisdom by asking it questions beyond our own concerns. I call these "soul questions" after the first such reading I did, in which I asked the Shining Woman Tarot "What is soul?" (The answer was the Ace of Birds.) For this example I chose the Greenwood Tarot of Chesca Potter and Mark Ryan.

what is tarot?

Three of Cups – "Joy." Three herons spread their plumage around the prehistoric triple spiral of Ireland, symbol for many of the Triple goddess of the Celts. The text says "Celebration within a communal group or family, welcoming the coming new life or good fortune." Tarot is above all positive, a celebration of life, and even though we mostly work with it alone, it is a communal experience, based on centuries of dedication to symbolic truth.

The triple spiral of Ireland, symbol of the Triple goddess of the Celts.

where does it come from?

The Blasted Oak. This Major Arcana card links the Hanged Man – "divine sacrifice" – and the Tower, "shattered by the storm" that "cleans and burns away illusion." This picture reminds us that whatever the historical origins of the Tarot, its use in divination takes its "true" origin back to the prophetic revelations of the seers and shamans. The text says, "What appears to be a total and random dissolution of your beliefs and relationships is timely and natural." With the Tarot, what appeared originally as a random collection of allegorical pictures emerged into a system of self-knowledge.

The Three of Cups as it appears in the Greenwood Tarot.

Three of Cups

Joy

how does it teach us?

Page of Wands – "Stoat." The court cards in the Greenwood deck use animals. The stoat has a "fierce

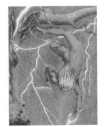

The Blasted Oak

The Blasted Oak, from the Greenwood Tarot.

The Tarot requires that we hunt the truth under the "Moon" of instinct.

hunting instinct" and an "ability to live underground." The Tarot "hunts" the truth by taking us underneath our surface knowledge and beliefs. In that first reading when I asked the question, "What is soul?", the Ace of Birds implied that the soul is a hunter of wisdom in the dark night of experience.

what are tarot readings?

The Archer. This is another Major card. This picture describes readings as arrows aimed at concealed truth – they are concealed both because the events lie in the future, but also because they are concealed by our own blindness to our real selves. The book connects the card to the Chariot. Readings are an act of will coming from a desire to know. The Archer is female. That, together with the attendant dogs, marks her as Artemis/Diana, a goddess of the Moon, and therefore of intuitive leaps of understanding. As with readings, "The key to a smooth and accurate release of the arrow is a steady and relaxed state, both physical and mental."

how do they work?

Seven of Arrows (Swords) – "Insecurity." This frightening supernatural image reminds us that the majority of people seek readings in times of anxiety, worry, and hope. In short, during times of great insecurity. The readings "work" because in this heightened state we are then pushed beyond our normal skepticism and our habitual ways of looking at our lives. (A skeptic might point out that the picture on the Seven of Arrows depicts illusions, and say that readings don't work at all. We just project our own fantasies onto the pictures. This would be a paradox, since this card of illusion comes in a reading.)

how do we use them?

Three of Wands – "Fulfillment." The Tarot comes from the shattering of the Blasted Oak. It works through our insecurities and requires that we hunt the truth under the "Moon" of instinct. At heart, however, it remains the "Joy" of the Three of Cups. And we use readings best when we are able to heal and "fulfill" ourselves. The text for this card says, "Nourishment from a spiritual source that gives inner security and joy." We use readings when we allow the cards to nourish us and resolve the deep insecurities that sent us to them in the first place.

There are no "correct" answers to these kinds of questions. Do them with your own deck and see what truths you can hunt.

The Archer

The powerful female Archer looks about to release her arrow at the Moon.

Stoat

Page of Wands

Seven of Arrows

Insecurity

Three of Wands

Fulfilment

The Court Cards in the Greenwood Tarot follow the prehistoric link of human and animal.

Sometimes we determine that certain cards, or rather the qualities they signify, are just what we need. We may decide this from a reading, or simply by looking through the deck until we click on a particular image. Obviously, we want to do more than say to ourselves, "I sure wish I could stay calm, like Temperance," or "I wish I had more Chariot will-power." These are qualities. We also might want to bring about a certain result. "I want Bill to fall in love with me and make the Two of Cups come true," or "Why can't the Ace of Pentacles come out of the cloud with money for me?"

ways to work with a card

41

To help wishes come about involves a combination of direct action and magic. We will look at the magic part in a moment. For now, we want to see how you can work with the qualities of a particular card to change yourself and in so doing bring about change in your life.

One simple way to do this is to carry the card around with you. Put it someplace where you will see it regularly, such as your wallet or appointment book. When you see the card you can take the opportunity to say to yourself, "This Chariot will help me focus my will," or "This Two of Cups will help me open myself to love." From time to time during the day hold it in your hand, close your eyes, and focus on the qualities that the card symbolizes for you.

You can go further to make the card real by small physical acts that will emphasize its value. These do not have to mean any bizarre behavior. For example, if the color yellow dominates the picture you might choose to wear something yellow each day you work on the card. For a class that I held one year in January, I developed the idea of choosing a card for a New Year's Resolution. The card I chose for myself, the Gift of Rivers from the Shining Woman Tarot, shows a fish goddess dancing before a snake. Over the

Carry your card around with you in your pocket, wallet or in a special pouch.

Wear items, such as a necklace or earrings, that symbolize your chosen card.

next week I wrote about this card in my journal, meditated on it, and performed a ritual with it. But I also tried to do some of the more joyous activities that the card symbolized, and wore such items as fish-shaped earrings, or a necklace engraved with a snake.

At the start of this period write down what you understand of the card. At the end of the day, read it through and see what fresh insights come to you. Write these down as well. Include all the ways in which you could apply the card in your life. You might find that you begin negatively – the ways you do not have the things you desire. Make a deliberate effort to find positive evidence. Over the next few days, when you return to your journal, see if such evidence has become clearer.

You can enhance your positive outlook over a longer period of time through affirmations. Affirmations are statements that you make about yourself to imprint the qualities and beliefs that you want. They work from the idea that we unconsciously tell ourselves "scripts" about who we are, over and over. These scripts often carry destructive beliefs, such as, "I'm ugly, no one will ever love me," or "I just fail at everything I do." Affirmations allow us to counter such beliefs consciously, until they eventually sink to the unconscious level.

Write down the qualities you like about the card. Then make them into a statement about yourself. For example, you might write of the Lovers, "They express their passion openly and freely. They allow love to flow between them. The angels bless their love." You could then write something like, "I express my passion. Love blesses my life." Make sure the affirmation is positive. Not "I am not afraid of the future," but "I look to the future joyously." Repeat your affirmation several times each morning and evening. Some people write it on a card and tape it to the bathroom mirror so they will see it when they first get up. Never mind if you don't believe it when you begin, or even if it embarrasses you. Try it as an experiment over several weeks and see what happens. Someone once described an affirmation as a lie we tell ourselves until it becomes true.

Now phrase the qualities of a card into a statement about yourself.

The Lovers

Repeat your affirmation when you see it taped to the mirror

The heart, symbol of love

Write down the card's qualities spontaneously, and make them into a statement about yourself

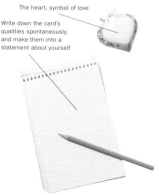

Meditation allows us to engage the pictures on the cards in a very direct way. There are many forms of meditation. We will look at a "program" that will allow you to enter and explore any card.

meditation with the tarot

We begin with relaxation. A relaxed state allows you to step outside the usual movement of your life. Choose a place where you can sit comfortably so that you will not have to shift around, but try to sit with your back straight. Place the card you want to explore close by so you can easily pick it up. Since you do not want to stop and consult this book, or even have to remind yourself what comes next, you might want to make a tape of the following directions. Speak softly, without rush.

Sit comfortably, keep your eyes closed and your back straight.

When you have found a comfortable position close your eyes. Feel that you are coming to a rest, still. Let thoughts and plans and problems begin to slide away from you. Begin to breathe deeply and easily. Allow the breath to go right the way down to the center of your body. As you take a breath out, release it entirely, in the confidence that your next breath will be there for you when you are ready for it. (Brief pause).

As you breathe in, breathe in a deep calm all through your body. Let it radiate through you. And as you breathe out, let the breath carry away any distractions or worries.

And as you breathe in, let your breath bring you the light of the stars. Let it fill you, shine in you. You are a creature of light. And when you breathe out, send the light down into the Earth. Send it through the floor, the dirt, the rock, deep into the Earth. With each breath you become a link between the stars and the Earth. (Pause).

Now, with your eyes closed, and staying with your breath, reach out for the card. Hold it in both hands and feel its energy. Quietly open your eyes and look at it. See it as if for the first time. Absorb all the details, colors, and characters. When you have seen it fully, close your eyes again and visualize the card in front of you. (Brief pause).

Open your eyes and look again. What details did you miss? What small form or gesture did you leave out? Now close your eyes again and set down the card. Once more see it before you. Let the picture become bigger, the size of a large book, then a window. And bigger still, until it becomes like a doorway. A doorway to a living world.

Hold the card in both hands and feel the energy.

Motionless, with your eyes closed, imagine yourself standing before that doorway. Now you step through it. Now you find yourself inside that world.

Let yourself look around. The world has grown beyond the picture. Feel the ground, the breezes, smell the air, hear any noises of birds or people or wind. (Brief pause).

As you look around, you see the characters from the original picture. They are active now, and you watch them move and speak. (Pause).

Now you find yourself drawn to them. You approach them and one figure, a person, or animal, or object, draws you still closer. You feel a special bond with this figure, this ally. Allow yourself to explore that. (Pause).

And now this powerful figure asks you to come very close. You approach the figure and the being offers you a precious gift. Allow yourself to discover this gift and accept it. (Pause). Now you give your ally a gift in return. (Brief pause).

Writing your experiences in a journal will open fresh awareness.

You recognize that the time has come to leave. You say goodbye to your ally and let yourself step back. As you move away the scene becomes the way it was when you first entered it. You look and see the doorway behind you. You step backward through it, so that the scene once more lies on the other side. And now that doorway begins to shrink – the size of a window, a large book, a card. Now the picture you have created dissolves before you.

Sit quietly a moment, then take a deep breath, and when you let it out open your eyes.Write or draw in your journal what you have experienced.

MEDITATION TO MOVE THROUGH THE CARDS

Meditation on the Fool will open you to the dance of freedom.

The previous meditation provided a storyline for you to encounter a card. You can do a more general meditation by using your breath to enter into the special quality of a card. For the Fool, you might open yourself to become unattached to old rules or beliefs, free to dance in any direction. For the Magician, you could see yourself in radiant light, a channel for power to make life happen. The High Priestess would call you to descend into stillness, conscious of mystery with no need to explain anything.

You can use this style of meditation to enter more than one card in a session. Set out a small number – three works well – on the floor or table. You might choose the Fool, the Magician, and the High Priestess, with the Fool in the middle and slightly above the others. Enter the meditative state and when you feel at peace, open your eyes slightly to focus on the Fool. Close your eyes again and breathe into the spirit of the card. That is, with each breath you go more fully into that experience of freedom and wonder. Then, when you want to shift, release the card, thank it in your mind, and then open your eyes briefly to focus on the Magician. Let your breath take you into his power and radiance. Once more, release the card and now move to the High Priestess. When you have experienced all three cards, return simply to your breath. Sit for a few moments in peace and quiet, and then with a final breath open your eyes.

You can do this card-shifting in an open style, with intuition to tell you when to move on to the next card. Or, you might prefer a system where you will not have to think about when to change. One such system involves counting breaths. When you have found your inner awareness, take five full breaths. Breathe deeply but easily, and with each breath let yourself go deeper into the world of the cards as a whole. After the fifth breath open your eyes to the first card. Now take 10 breaths, each one a passage deeper into the picture and its special truth. After 10 breaths, sit quietly a moment. Do 10 breaths for each further card. Finally, count five more breaths to bring yourself back to ordinary consciousness. It may sound artificial to count

You may want to use more than one card for your meditation. Side cards can support the central image and its qualities.

your breath. Paradoxically, many people find it takes them very deeply into the cards.

You can use this kind of meditation to work with a "mandala" based on cards from a reading. Return for a moment to the Sample Celtic Cross *(see page 311).* To make a mandala, the person first chooses a card she considers vital to what she hopes will come out of the reading. In this case the woman chose the High Priestess, for her ability to love and forgive without losing her detachment. Now look for cards that will give support to the basic issue. The woman chose both two Queens, the Significator Queen of Pentacles for her earthiness and the Queen of Wands (Recent Past) for her optimism. These qualities prevent the High Priestess from emotional withdrawal. We placed these cards on either side to balance and support the central card.

Next look for a card that can symbolize long-range goals. For the woman, this was the Ten of Cups. Though its vision of a happy family appeared unrealistic at the moment she still hoped for this at some time in her life. This went above the High Priestess.

Buddhist mandalas code great depths of teachings into harmonious designs.

With this arrangement you can meditate through the cards by starting at the center then moving out to the support cards, then back to the center. You also can look at the mandala in a more conventionally accepted way, thinking about the relationships between the cards, the issues they illustrate, how the connections between the various cards change and how this amplifies the individual messages.

The mandala cards helped the woman create a clear vision of her desire for love.

You've done the reading, you've determined what changes you would like to see in yourself and in your life. You can use meditation or a journal to understand the cards better. Can you also use the cards as magic, to change reality itself?

magic and tarot

Ritual magicians, such as the heirs to the Hermetic Order of the Golden Dawn, define magic as the ability to change the outer world according to the magician's will and not to the magician's desire, because desire remains an idle fantasy.

Magic calls for a quite deliberate act. This definition does not require belief in spirits or demons or anything supernatural. Magicians may in fact believe that their rituals allow them to contact spirit beings on the "astral plane" but this is not the central issue. Focused will remains the core of magic.

Join deeply with the card before turning it around.

The Tarot can help us to train and exercise our will. When we read the Tarot cards we understand ourselves and the forces that shape us, an essential part of the will, for how can you direct energy without self-knowledge? And the cards give us images and symbols we can use to focus our sometimes vague intentions.

Consider the following situation. You've done a reading that shows all the issues, but the cards have come out the wrong way around. That is, the Eight of Swords signifies your feelings of helplessness and confusion. You would rather see it reversed as a sign that you have begun to

Swords/Air can go in the north.

Wands/Fire can go in the east.

liberate yourself and taken the first steps toward a new life. By contrast, the Ten of Cups, the card that represents everything you desire, does come out reversed, a symbol of all that life seems to deny you. What would happen if you turned them around? If you did it flippantly, it would demonstrate nothing more than wishful thinking. But suppose you did it with great intention, as a way to reach out and reshape reality itself?

We have seen how a Tarot reading forms a symbolic picture of the web of influences that bind us to the world. Imagine that that picture is not static, but bears a living relationship to what happens in your life. If you change the picture, can you change the situation? So before you turn the cards you breathe deeply, as in meditation, send yourself down into the underlying web of patterns, and only then reach out to turn them around. Thus an idle gesture becomes an act of magic.

More elaborate magical acts usually work through rituals. The ritual allows us to raise our energy and our will to the point where our stated intentions take on the power to change ourselves and our world. Books on magic (and classes and workshops) will give you detailed instructions on how to conduct a ritual. Briefly, you want to open a "sacred space," that is to say, the sense that the place and time where you do the ritual stands apart from ordinary life. You can do this by setting out candles, burning incense or a "smudge stick" (herbal bundles that give off purifying smoke), meditation and deep breathing, chanting, drumming, or other rhythmic sounds, calling out names of gods and goddesses, and so on.

One way to use the cards in this process is to set out the four Aces to signify the four directions and their elements. Not everyone agrees on which elements go where. One such arrangement is to put Wands/Fire in the east, Cups/Water in the south, Swords/Air in the north, and Pentacles/Earth in the west. As you set them out you call the spirit of the direction and element to aid your ritual.

Cups/Water can go in the south.

When you have opened the space you can perform the ritual itself. With the cards that you choose, you can create a picture of a reality. You will want to choose the cards ahead of time. Choose them deliberately, not randomly as in a reading. They signify what your will seeks to bring into existence. Narrow your focus to a single issue – the Two of Cups, with cards to support it, rather than the Two of Cups and the Ace of Pentacles and the World. The supporting cards should give detail to the basic vision. The clearer you can see it the more real you can make it.

Pentacles/Earth can go in the west.

With the cards set out, call on your spirit allies to help you bring the vision into the world. Use magical tools and gestures (for example, the Magician posture with a wand to channel energy into reality) to help seal the ritual.

At the end, thank and release whatever beings have helped you, then close your sacred space and return the cards to the deck.

We have looked at Tarot through many lenses in this book. We have seen its mystic origins, its many myths and secrets. We have explored its symbols, its allegories, its moral lessons. We have seen its visions of spiritual enlightenment and we have discovered how these simple pictures open up worlds of wonder, from the mystic lights of the Kabbalistic *sephiroth*, to gods and goddesses of many cultures, to practices and beliefs of people all over the world, to the sky patterns of stars and planets, to the transformations of alchemy.

final words –
a life in the cards

We have seen how a reading can describe reality and a ritual can change it. We have seen readings that show us our past and future, readings that show us our challenges, readings that describe our relationships, our spiritual quests, our history with our parents and our future with our lovers. We have asked the cards about the mysteries of the soul, we have explored the world's stories and our own dreams. We have created our own pictures and told our own stories.

The Tarot is like a portable Tree of Knowledge.

The Tarot is a small world of its own and one that opens pathways to much greater worlds. Remember the story of Paul Foster Case, the founder of the Builders of the Adytum – "Say, Case, where do you suppose playing cards come from?"

With the same kind of innocent curiosity, we enter the world of Tarot – and our lives change. Once the pictures have drawn us in and begun to reveal their symbolic secrets, we discover how much the cards can teach us, how much we can learn about ourselves.

Discover the many worlds that you can enter in just three cards.

An old saying describes an event as "in the cards." Ordained. Predestined. Inevitable. We have seen how the cards show us likely futures but they do not compel us. They do not take away free will, they increase it through awareness.

But we can, however, look at that expression, "in the cards," in a different way. It describes the endless possibilities that open up for us when we enter into the world of Tarot.

A life in the cards is a life of discovery. A life of knowledge and excitement. It is a life of tradition, with all the ideas and images people have poured into the Tarot over the centuries, but also a life of invention and change, for the Tarot constantly evolves, constantly explores new territory. A life in the cards is truly a life of wonder.

glossary

Albigensians a heretical Gnostic group in France in the era before the appearance of the first known Tarot decks.

Alchemy an ancient science that attempted to turn base metals into gold. Many alchemists understood their quest as personal transformation. Alchemical images may have influenced the development of Tarot.

Arcana Latin for "secrets."

Baphomet supposed idol of the Knights Templar. The depiction of the Devil in the Tarot is often based on Baphomet.

Bembo Bonifacio probable painter of some of the earliest known Tarot decks, including the Visconti-Sforza.

Book of Thoth name given by Aleister Crowley to the deck he designed, painted during World War II by Lady Frieda Harris. The name derives from a supposed book of all knowledge given by the God Thoth to his human disciples.

BOTA Builders of the Adytum, a post-Golden Dawn group started by Paul Foster Case. Their correspondence course has greatly influenced modern Tarot.

Divination any method of creating patterns to gain knowledge that is not available by ordinary means.

Dualism the idea that the universe is composed of opposites, such as light and dark, good and evil, life and death. For many, the spiritual goal of Tarot is to harmonize such seeming contradictions.

Elements basic qualities of existence. In Tarot (and also in astrology), these are Fire, Water, Air, and Earth.

Eliot, T. S. Nobel-prize winning poet. His most famous poem, "The Wasteland," uses the Grail legend, and features a Tarot reader as one of the characters.

Etteila early French occultist, creator of the Grand Etteila Tarot.

Freemasonry an esoteric system using complex rituals. The Rider Pack contains a great deal of Masonic imagery.

Gnosticism branch of early Christianity that later became labeled a heresy. It taught that the soul is "imprisoned" in the physical world and that the way to liberation lies through "gnosis," or knowledge.

Heresy religious ideas that go against the official teachings of the Church.

Hermeticism esoteric philosophy of self-transformation, attributed to a legendary ancient philosopher, Hermes Trismegistus.

Hermetic Order of the Golden Dawn Magical group from the end of the 19th century. Its synthesis of vast amounts of esoteric information used the Tarot as the symbolic key.

Holy Grail supposed cup which Christ used at the Last Supper. The Grail symbolizes perfection. Some consider the Grail imagery the source of the Tarot, especially the four suits.

I Ching both a book and an ancient Chinese method of divination. Sticks and coins are used to create a "hexagram" which the diviner then looks up in the text.

Ifa a traditional West African form of divination. Ifa is both a method for individual guidance and the way the Orishas, or Gods, make themselves known to humans.

Kabbalah collective term for Jewish mystical magical teachings. Many consider it the origin of Tarot. Also spelled Qabala, Cabala, etc.

Knights Templar order of knights originally formed to protect pilgrims in Palestine. Their enemies accused them of occult practices, including divination and the worship of a demon called Baphomet.

Le Monde Primitif a massive 18th-century work by Antoine Court de Gébelin. It contained the first mention of the Tarot as a secret doctrine from Ancient Egypt.

Meditation a method of stilling the mind and the body to gain spiritual awareness.

Major Arcana the twenty-two named and numbered cards that distinguish Tarot from ordinary playing cards. They symbolize large spiritual issues.

Minor Arcana the four suits of the Tarot. Each suit contains Ace–Ten, plus Page, Knight, Queen, and King.

Querent the person who seeks a reading.

Reader the person who lays out the cards and interprets them.

Rider Pack the world's most popular Tarot deck, designed by Arthur Edward Waite and painted by Pamela Colman Smith. The name "Rider" comes from its original publisher, who brought it out in 1910.

Sephiroth **(singular,** *sephirah*) ten circles of divine energy that form the Tree of Life.

Suits the four parts of the Minor Arcana. Each suit carries specific qualities and is related to one of the four Elements. The names of the suits vary greatly in modern Tarot. Following are the most common:

Cups – Water – love, emotion, fantasy, dreams.

Pentacles (also called Coins, or Disks) – Earth – money, nature, work, home.

Swords – Air – mind, conflict, sorrow.

Wands (also called Staves) – energy, action, enthusiasm.

Taras manifestations of the Goddess in the Tantric religion of India.

Taro River a river in Northern Italy, near the region of the first known Tarot decks.

Tarocchi the original Italian name for the Tarot cards and the game played with them. The name is of uncertain origin.

Tarock an Austrian version of Tarocchi, usually played with a shorter deck.

further reading

Historical

Decker, Ronald and Depaulis, Thierry, and Dummett, Michael, *A Wicked Pack of Cards,* St. Martins, 1996

Douglas, Alfred, *The Tarot: The Origins, Meaning and Uses of the Cards,* Penguin, 1972

Dummett, Michael, *The Game of Tarot,* U.S. Games Systems, 1980

Huson, Paul, *The Devil's Picturebook,* G.P. Putnam's Sons, 1971

Kaplan, Stuart, *The Encyclopedia of Tarot,* U.S. Games Systems, 1990

Mathers, S.L., *Tarot,* Gordon, 1973

Moakley, Gertrude, *The Tarot Cards Painted by Bonifacio Bembo,* New York Public Library, 1966

O'Neill, Robert V., *Tarot Symbolism,* Fairways Press, 1986

Wang, Robert, *Introduction to the Golden Dawn Tarot,* Samuel Weiser, 1978

Interpretive

Anonymous, *Meditations on the Tarot,* Element Books, 1985

Case, Paul Foster, *The Tarot,* Builders of the Adytum, 1974

Connolly, Eileen, *Tarot: A New Handbook for the Apprentice,* Newcastle, 1979

Connolly, Eileen, *Tarot: A New Handbook for the Journeyman,* Newcastle, 1979

Crowley, Aleister, *The Book of Thoth,* U.S. Games Systems, 1977

Fairfield, Gail, *Choice-centered Tarot,* Newcastle, 1985

Gearhart, Sally and Rennie, Susan, *A Feminist Tarot,* Persephone, 1977

Gray, Eden, *Complete Guide to the Tarot,* Bantam, 1971

Greer, Mary K., *Tarot for Yourself,* Newcastle, 1984

Greer, Mary K., *Tarot Constellations,* Newcastle, 1988

Greer, Mary K., *Tarot Mirrors,* Newcastle, 1988

Lotterhand, Jason C., *Thursday Night Tarot,* Newcastle, 1989

Nichols, Sallie, *Jung and Tarot,* Samuel Weiser, 1981

Noble, Vicki, *Motherpeace: A Way to the Goddess Through Myth, Art, and Tarot,* Harper and Row, 1983

Pollack, Rachel, *78 Degrees of Wisdom, Part One,* Aquarian, 1980

Pollack, Rachel, *78 Degrees of Wisdom, Part Two,* Aquarian, 1983

Pollack, Rachel, *Shining Woman Tarot,* Thorsons, 1994

Pollack, Rachel, *Tarot Readings and Meditations,* Aquarian, 1986

Riley, Jana, *Tarot Dictionary and Compendium,* Samuel Weiser, 1995

Waite, A.E., *The Pictorial Key to the Tarot,* Samuel Weiser, 1983

Wang, Robert, *Qabalistic Tarot,* Samuel Weiser, 1983

index

Cards are indexed at the terminology used in the Waite decks, with cross references to these terms from designations used in other decks. Page numbers in *italics* indicate illustrations. Page numbers in **bold** indicate main entries. Main entries for individual cards include discussion of card symbolism, imagery, interpretation etc for several different decks; such discussion has not normally been indexed separately.

The publishers wish to thank the following for the use of pictures

Archiv für Kunst und Geschichte, London: pp. 47 (Bibliothèque de L'Arsenal), 113l & 113r (Bibliothèque Estense, Modena), 160 (India House Office), 200, 216, 260, 270, 300, 389. AKG/Herbert Kraft: p. 13t. AKG London/Erich Lessing: pp. 57t (Judaica Coll. Max Berger, Vienna), 188 (Museum Pomorskie, Danzig), 196 (Jucaica Coll. Max Berger, Vienna), 295 (Uffizi), 321. Bridgeman Art Library, London: 2 Warburg Institute), 34, 37, 45 (Phillips), 65, 73bl (Warburg Institute), 183, 276. Cameron Collection: p. 148. Mary Evans Picture Library: pp. 52, 59b. e.t.archive: pp. 39, 180 (Tate Gallery), 220br, 283. Fortean Picture Library: p. 72. Sonia Halliday: p. 30. Images Colour Library: pp. 12t, 64, 119, 272, 281. The Image Bank: pp.81, 132, 165, 336, 337. The Kobal Collection: pp. 172. The Stock Market: pp. 105, 106, 109, 150, 186, 230, 335, 370b. Trip/Mender: p. 131bl.

Illustrations from the following decks reproduced by permission of US Games Systems Inc., Stamford, CT 06902 USA. Further reproduction prohibited.

Astrological Tarot © 1983 pp. 112t, 112b. Barbara Walker Tarot © 1986 pp. 303b. Cary-Yale Visconti Tarot © 1985 pp. 43t, 43b, 158, 162tl, 277t. Tarot of Ceremonial Magic © 1994 pp. 128, 181br. Egipcios Kier Tarot © 1984 pp. 80t, 169br. Golden Dawn Tarot © 1982 pp. 19t, 21, 66l, 66c, 66r, 69t, 70c, 95, 101, 102t, 102b, 103, 129b, 131, 164l, 204, 244r, 245b, 257b, 262r, 263r, 265l, 310t, 310c, 310b, 311 (all cards), 385. Haindl Tarot © 1991 pp. 41l, 127, 151, 162c, 169l, 174r, 179cr, 243b, 247t, 251, 252r, 256b, 257t, 258r, 262l, 277c, 302l, 302c, 302r. Herbal Tarot © 1990 p. 124. 1J Swiss Tarot © 1974 p. 380. Tarot of Marseilles © 1986/Carta Mundi pp. 17t, 19b, 70l, 83 (all cards), 107 (all cards), 143, 145, 147l, 149r, 153, 155b, 156, 179tl, 190, 241, 245, 250r, 271r, 274b, 278t, 293, 307 (all cards), 348, 375t. Morgan-Greer Tarot © 1993 pp. 40, 137, 139 (all cards), 141 (all cards), 174t, 187br, 271t, 271b, 349, 352 (all cards), 354 (all), 355. The Royal Fez Moroccan Tarot © 1975 p. 38. Motherpeace Tarot © 1996/Motherpeace Inc. 1981, 1983 pp. 25, 149c, 175, 184br, 277b. Oswald Wirth Tarot © 1976 pp. 81b, 173, 381l, 381cl, 381r. Papus Tarot © 1983 p. 33r. Renaissance Tarot © 1997. Tavaglione Stairs of Gold Tarot © 1982 p. 23. Tarot of the Spirit © 1996 pp. 179tr, 301l, 301cl, 301r. Ukiyoé Tarot © 1983 pp. 24t, 159r, 330, 331r, 331l, 357l, 357r. Universal Waite Tarot © 1990 pp. 20, 51, 70br, 79, 84r, 84l, 85r, 85l, 96r, 96b, 97, 121b, 133t, 147r, 149tl, 154, 157, 159c, 163, 167l, 171b, 177, 194tl, 197t, 197b, 198, 199t, 199b, 201l, 202t, 202b, 203l, 205b, 205l, 206t, 207l, 208b, 209t, 211l, 211, 212b, 213b, 214t, 215t, 217t, 218t, 219b, 220t, 222b, 223t, 225, 227b, 228t, 228b, 229t, 231, 232t, 233t, 234t, 235t, 237b, 238t, 239t, 242t, 247b, 248t, 249l, 250b, 252l, 253l, 254l, 256t, 258t, 259l, 263l, 264l, 265r, 319 (all cards), 345b, 363b, 363bl. Visconti-Sforza Tarot © 1975 pp. 17b, 144, 168, 187tl, 193, 347, 362 (all cards), 363tl, 363tll. Alchemical Tarot © HarperCollins Publishers Ltd, UK. pp. 184c, 195b, 201c, 206b, 207c, 212t, 221, 229c, 235t, 255, 386t, 386b, 387t, 387b, 390 (all cards). The Aleister Crowley Thoth Tarot* : Illustrations reproduced by permission of AGM AGMüller, CH-8212 Neuhausen, Switzerland. Further reproduction prohibited. © AGM, Switzerland/OTO, USA. pp. 73 (all cards), 111

(all cards), 152, 159l, 176, 187c, 194b, 208t, 213t, 214b, 215b, 217b, 218b, 220b, 222t, 223b, 224b, 227t, 228c, 229b, 232b, 233b, 234b, 237b, 243t, 248r, 253r, 264r, 278b. The Angels Tarot © Robert Michael Place/HarperCollins Publishers Ltd, UK p. 120 (all cards). The Arthurian Tarot: © Caitlín and John Matthews/HarperCollins Publishers Ltd, UK. pp. 41r, 323 (all cards). De Hierofant's Alchemisten Tarot: De Hierofant, Steenweg op Heindonk 34, 2801 Heffen-Mechelen. pp. 48r, 481. BOTA (Builders of the Adytum): Grateful acknowledgment is made to Builders of the Adytum, 5105 N. Figueroa Street, Los Angeles CA 90042, USA for permission to use their Tarot Keys. The permission granted for the use of materials of Builders of the Adytum, Incorporated, in no way endorses the material presented in this book. pp. 75, 358 (all cards), 361 (all cards). Charles VI Tarot: Bibliothèque National, Paris, France. pp. 13b, 184tl, 189t. Cosmo Tarot: © 1986 Carol Herzer, 4 Broadview Road, Woodstock NY 12498, USA. p. 114 (all cards). Elemental Tarot: © 1988 Caroline Smith, South Molton, North Devon, UK. pp. 15, 115 (all cards), 162r, 189b, 195t, 203r, 207t, 209b, 219t, 222c, 226t, 226b, 236b, 238bl, 239b. El Grand Tarot Esoterico: © Naipes Heraclio Fournier, Vitoria, Spain. pp. 49r, 164r, 181c, 191t, 211t. Grand Etteila Tarot: © J.M. Simon 1977. Ets. J.M. Simon-France-Cartes, 27 Avenue Pierre Lee de Serbie, 75116, Paris. p. 62 (all cards). Gipsy Tarot (Zigeuner): Illustrations reproduced by permission of AGM AGMüller, CH-8212 Neuhausen, Switzerland. Further reproduction prohibited. © AGM AGMüller, Switzerland. pp. 35, 49l. The Greenwood Tarot: © Mark Ryan and Chesca Potter/HarperCollins Publishers Ltd, UK. pp. 292, 369b, 370t, 371 (all cards). Tarot Jacques Vieville: Heron Boechat, Maitres Cartiers à Bordeaux, France. P 171t. Kashmir Tarot: Nicholas Van Beek, Balthasar Florisstraat 55, 1071 VB Amsterdam. Distributed by Outer Order Productions, P.O. Box 5461, Santa Monica, CA 90405, USA. p. 31. The Light and Shadow Tarot by Brian Williams and Michael Goepferd, published by Destiny Books, an imprint of Inner Traditions, Rochester, VT 05767, USA. Artwork copyright © 1997 by Michael Goepferd. pp. 167r, 312, 313, 314, 315 (all cards), 383 (all cards). The Merlin Tarot: © R. J. Stewart and Miranda Gray/HarperCollins Publishers Ltd, UK. p. 170. The Mythic Tarot: © Cards from the Mythic Tarot by Liz Green and Juliet Sharman-Burke published in the U.S. and Australia by Simon and Schuster and in the U.K. by Random House. Card artwork is copyright Tricia Newell. pp. 121t, 129t, 133b, 149c, 303t, 338–339(all cards). The New Golden Dawn Ritual Tarot by Sandra Tabatha Cicero: © 1991 Llewellyn Worldwide Ltd, P.O. Box 64383, Saint Paul, Minnesota 55164, USA. All rights reserved. pp. 69b, 71, PoMo: © Brian Williams/HarperCollins Publishers Ltd, UK. p. 24b. Shining Woman: © Rachel Pollack/HarperCollins Publishers Ltd, UK. pp. 155t, 181t, 327 (all cards), 367 (all cards). Transformational Tarot: © 1995 Foolscap Press, 1809 Ward Street, Berkeley, CA 94703, USA. p. 291. Tarot of Transition: © Carta Mundi of Belgium, Turnhout, Belgium. p. 33t. Voyager Tarot by James Wanless and Ken Knutson/Merrill-West Publications, Carmel CA, USA. pp 244l, 246, 249r, 254r, 259r. The Wheel of Change Tarot by Alexandra Genetti, published by Destiny Books, an imprint of Inner Traditions Internationa, Rochester, VT 05767, USA. Copyright © 1997 by Alexandra Genetti. pp. 98–99 (all cards), 296 (all cards), 297 (all cards), 299 (all cards). The William Blake Tarot: © Ed Buryn/HarperCollins Publishers Ltd, UK. pp. 343, 344 (all cards)